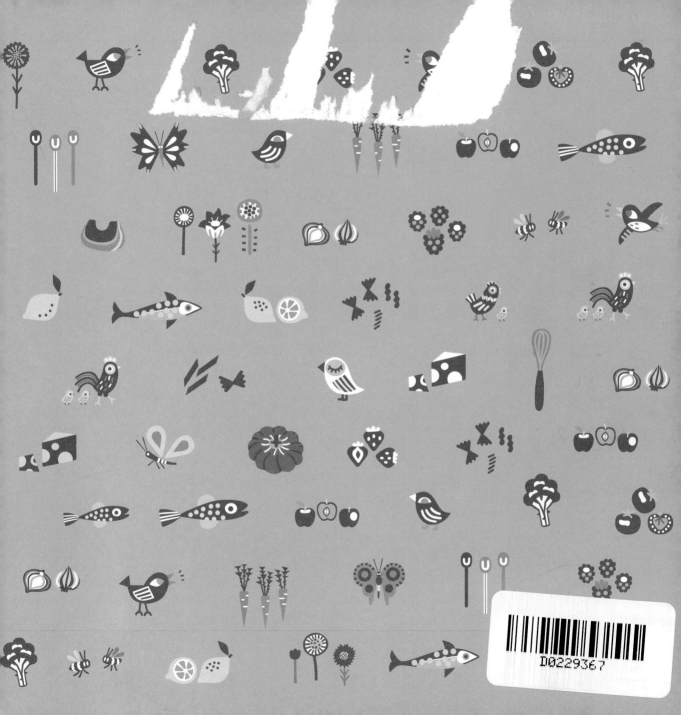

D0229367

annabel karmel

Quick and Easy
Toddler
Recipes

10 9 8 7 6 5 4 3 2 1

Published in 2013 by Ebury Press, an imprint of Ebury Publishing
A Random House Group Company

The Random House Group Limited Reg. No. 954009

A CIP catalogue record for this book is available from the British Library

The Random House Group Limited supports The Forest Stewardship
Council® (FSC®), the leading international forest-certification
organisation. Our books carrying the FSC label are printed on
FSC®-certified paper. FSC is the only forest-certification scheme supported
by the leading environmental organisations, including Greenpeace.
Our paper procurement policy can be found at
www.randomhouse.co.uk/environment

MIX
Paper from
responsible sources
FSC® C008047

Design by Smith & Gilmour
Photography by Dave King
(except page 45, Angus Muir)
Illustrations by Gwénola Carrère
Food styling by Maud Eden and Lizzie Harris
Prop styling by Tamsin Weston

Printed and bound in China
by C&C Offset Printing Co., Ltd

ISBN 978-0-09-194152-9

contents

Breakfasts
and Snacks

Fruit Porridge

A bowl of porridge at breakfast gives your child an energy boost that will keep them going right through the morning. If you think you don't have time to make porridge in the morning, think again; with this microwave recipe you'll be feeding your hungry bears in minutes!

Ingredients

Makes 3 portions

40 g (1½ oz) porridge oats
20 g (¾ oz) raisins or sultanas
250 ml (8 fl oz) milk
1 ripe banana
1 tsp honey

✳ Put the oats and raisins or sultanas into a bowl and pour over the milk. Cook in a 750W microwave for 4 minutes.

✳ Mash the banana and stir it into the cooked porridge, and drizzle over the honey to serve.

Red Smoothie

Kids love blitzing up fruit to make their own fresh and tasty smoothie, so get them involved in making this healthy breakfast drink.

Ingredients

Makes 1 glass

100 g (3½ oz) strawberries, quartered
100 g (3½ oz) raspberries
2 pots blueberry yoghurt
    (such as mini
    Actimel yoghurt drinks)
1 tbsp maple syrup

✳ Measure all of the ingredients into a jug, then blend them together using a hand blender until smooth. Serve chilled.

Cleaning up
Keep the kitchen sink full of soapy water and put the dirty utensils in as you cook for easy cleaning.

Ingredients

200 g (7 oz) self-raising flour
50 g (2 oz) light brown sugar
1 tsp baking powder
1 egg
1 x 234 ml pot of buttermilk
1 tsp vanilla extract
a pinch of salt
200 g (7 oz) blueberries
a little oil or butter, for frying
maple syrup and butter,
    to serve

Buttermilk Blueberry Pancakes

Frying pancakes in butter gives them a richer flavour, but you can use a mix of butter and oil instead to prevent them sticking to the pan. This recipe makes 15 pancakes; for a smaller batch, either halve the ingredients or freeze the extras – separate them with baking parchment, wrap them in foil and put them in the freezer for up to one month.

✳ Put the flour, sugar and baking powder into a large mixing bowl. In another bowl, mix the egg and buttermilk together, then pour into the flour mixture. Add the vanilla and salt and whisk everything together until it makes a smooth batter. Tip in the blueberries and gently fold them evenly through the batter.

✳ Heat a little oil or butter in a frying pan until it is really hot, then ladle in 2 tablespoons of the batter, swirling it a little to create a pancake shape. Fry the pancakes for 2–3 minutes each side until lightly golden and puffy. Repeat until you have used up all the batter. Serve them with maple syrup and butter.

Makes 1
portion

Ingredients

1 large egg
1 tbsp milk
½ tomato, deseeded and diced
2 tsp chopped fresh basil
2 tbsp grated Parmesan
a knob of butter, for frying

Tomato and Basil Omelette

Eggs are an excellent source of protein, vitamins and iron and are brilliant for rustling up a speedy meal. In this recipe the tomato and basil add a fresh, delicious flavour.

✳ Mix the egg and milk together in a bowl. Add the tomato, basil and Parmesan cheese. Season to taste.

✳ Melt the butter in a small frying pan. Add the egg mixture, swirl it around the pan then leave it to cook for 2–3 minutes. Flip the omelette over and cook it on the other side for 1–2 minutes. Flip it out onto a plate and serve immediately.

Toast Toppings

These toppings are delicious on freshly made toast. For really crunchy toast, once it is made, let it stand in a toast rack for a minute or two, or prop the tops of two slices against each other in a triangle shape, to let it crisp up – the escaping steam will stop the toast becoming soggy.

Welsh Rarebit

The cheese mixture can be refrigerated for up to one day before using.

Ingredients

2 tbsp milk
100 g (3½ oz) Cheddar, grated
2–3 drops Worcestershire sauce
1 large egg yolk
2 slices unbuttered toast

✻ Put the milk in a small saucepan and heat gently, then add a handful of cheese and stir until the cheese has melted. Repeat with another handful, then add the rest and stir again. Remove the pan from the heat and stir in the Worcestershire sauce. Leave to cool to room temperature, then stir in the egg yolk.

✻ Preheat the grill to high and set the rack one shelf down from normal. Spread the cheese mixture thinly on the toast and put it under the grill for 1–2 minutes until the cheese is puffed and golden brown. Watch it carefully – the egg makes the cheese brown very quickly. Serve immediately.

Tomato and Cheese

Ingredients

1 slice toast, lightly buttered
1 tomato, thinly sliced
   (skinned, if you wish)
50 g (2 oz) Cheddar, grated

✻ Preheat the grill to high. Lay the tomato on the toast, overhanging the crust slightly so that the crust doesn't burn on grilling. Season with a little pepper, then scatter over the cheese evenly. Grill for 1½–2 minutes until the cheese is bubbling and turning brown.

Easy with the cheese
To save time buy ready-grated cheese.

Scrambled Eggs with Tomato Salsa on English Muffin

Makes 2 portions

Kids love scrambled eggs, and with a dollop of fresh tomato salsa this makes a hearty breakfast. If you want this for a quick lunch, try it served inside a tortilla wrap.

✳ Slice the muffin in half and toast the two halves in the toaster.

✳ Meanwhile, make the salsa. Mix all of the salsa ingredients together in a small bowl and season.

✳ In a small bowl, beat the eggs with the milk and season. Melt the butter in a pan, and when it starts to sizzle, pour in the egg mixture. Immediately reduce the heat to medium/low and sprinkle the eggs with a little salt and pepper to taste. Stir gently, and cook over the heat for 2–3 minutes until the eggs look wet but are no longer liquid. Remove the pan from the heat.

✳ Butter the toasted muffin halves and place on a plate. Top them with the scrambled eggs and then a little of the salsa.

Ingredients

1 English muffin
2 eggs
2 tbsp milk
a knob of butter, for cooking, plus extra for the toast

Salsa

1 tomato, deseeded and diced
2 thin spring onions, sliced
¼ red chilli (optional)
1 tbsp olive oil
½ tsp rice wine vinegar
1 tbsp chopped fresh basil

Boiled Egg and Soldiers

1 medium egg
1 slice bread
a knob of butter, for
    buttering the toast

Boiled egg with soldiers makes a great breakfast. Always check the date on your eggs to make sure that they are fresh. If you like you can spread the toast with a little Marmite.

✳ If your egg has been kept in the fridge it will need to warm up before you boil it, so put it in a saucepan of cold water and bring the water to the boil. If your egg is at room temperature, fill a saucepan three-quarters full of water and bring to the boil. Once it is boiling rapidly, gently lower the egg into the saucepan using a large spoon.

✳ As soon as the water comes to the boil and the eggs are immersed, set the timer to 4 minutes. This will give you a soft-boiled egg with a runny yolk.

✳ When your egg is done, lift it out of the pan using a slotted spoon. Set it in an egg cup and leave it to cool slightly before you break the top off with a spoon.

✳ Meanwhile, pop the bread in the toaster and cook until golden. Spread it with a little butter, cut it into 4 strips and serve alongside the egg.

Waffles with Summer Berries

Makes 2 portions

A delicious treat for breakfast
or at any time of day.

Ingredients

2 individual butter waffles
2 tbsp Greek yoghurt
a drizzle of honey
75 g (3 oz) summer berries
   (e.g. raspberries, blueberries, strawberries)

✱ Warm the waffles for 30 seconds in the microwave or in a toaster.

✱ Spoon the yoghurt over the waffles and drizzle them with honey. Arrange the berries on top.

Fresh Fruit Salad

Makes 3 portions

A chopped up piece of fruit might not tempt your child's tastebuds in the morning, but a colourful fruit salad might do the trick. Just one small bowl will help ensure your child gets his 5-a-day. (See photograph opposite.)

Ingredients

1 mango
2 oranges
150 g (5 oz) strawberries
150 g (5 oz) blueberries
2 tbsp caster sugar

✱ Peel the mango and remove the flesh from around the stone. Dice the fruit into 2½-cm (4-in) cubes and put in a mixing bowl.

✱ Peel and segment the oranges, then squeeze out the juice over the mango cubes. Hull and slice the strawberries and add to the bowl with the blueberries. Sprinkle over the caster sugar and mix everything together until evenly combined.

Quick Snacks

Kids need snacks between meals, but they shouldn't fill them up so they won't eat their main meal. Here are a few ideas for some simple, speedy snacks at any time of day.

★ Spread ½ tablespoon of cream cheese over a rice cake, then top with slices of tomato, cucumber or ham, or spoon over some mango chutney

★ Toast and slice up some pitta bread or chop up some vegetables and serve with a ready-made dip

★ Grill cheese and tomato on crumpets and slice into triangles

★ Fresh fruit

★ A handful of raisins, dried apricots, dried bananas or their favourite dried fruit

★ Cold Spanish omelette cut into little slices

★ Ham, mozzarella and cherry tomatoes threaded onto a straw

★ Tortilla topped with tomato salsa and cheese, grilled and cut into triangles

★ Toasted muffin or toasted sandwiches (see recipes on pages 11 and 18)

★ Milkshake or fruit smoothies

★ Toasted and sliced pitta bread with cream cheese and sweet chilli sauce

★ Mix mayonnaise with a little lemon juice and tomato ketchup and spread over a wrap. Scatter over some lettuce, chicken and quartered cherry tomatoes and roll up.

★ Mini bagels (they don't fall apart!)

★ Toast with peanut butter and banana

★ Popcorn

Sandwiches

Sandwiches can make a quick, easy and nutritious meal or snack, but sometimes you need some inspiration to ring the changes, so try some of these yummy fillings.

Hummus, Tomato and Cucumber

★ Lightly butter two slices of white bread, then spread 1 tablespoon of hummus on one slice. Top this with half a sliced tomato and 6 slices of cucumber. Top with the other piece of bread. Remove the crusts and slice the sandwich into 6 triangles or cut into fingers.

Peanut Butter and Banana

★ Spread 2 teaspoons of peanut butter on one slice of bread. Top with half a sliced banana and sandwich together with another slice of bread. Remove the crusts and slice into 6 triangles or fingers.

Mozzarella, Pesto, Avocado and Tomato

★ Lightly butter two slices of bread, then spread one piece with 2 teaspoons of pesto and top with 4 slices of mozzarella, a quarter of an avocado, sliced, and half a sliced tomato.

Sandwich together with the other piece of bread. Remove the crusts and cut the sandwich into 6 fingers.

Cream Cheese, Sweet Chilli and Cucumber

★ Lightly butter two slices of bread and spread one side with 1 tablespoon of cream cheese, such as Philadelphia. Spread the other side with 1 teaspoon of sweet chilli sauce. Top with 6 slices of cucumber. Sandwich together with the other piece of bread, remove the crusts and slice into 6 fingers.

Chicken and Sweetcorn

★ Mix together cooked chopped chicken, drained canned sweetcorn, sliced spring onion and 1 tablespoon of mayonnaise. Lightly butter two slices of bread and scatter some shredded lettuce over one side, top with the chicken mixture and cover with the remaining slice of bread. Remove the crusts and cut the sandwich in half.

Ingredients

2 slices wholemeal bread
a little butter, for spreading
1 slice ham
1 tomato, thinly sliced

Toasted Ham and Tomato Sandwiches

These always go down a treat as a quick snack during the day. If you like, you can vary the ingredients; other good options for fillings are cheese and tomato, ham and cheese or banana and peanut butter.

✷ Lightly butter the bread on both sides. Put the ham and tomato on one side and top with the other buttered slice to make a sandwich.

✷ Heat a frying pan until hot then fry the sandwiches on both sides for 2 minutes until brown and toasted. Slice into quarters or fingers, allow to cool a little, then serve.

Organise storage

Organise cupboards and drawers in the kitchen for easy access to frequently used equipment. Keep cooking utensils near your work surface, pots and pans near the stove and cleaning materials near the sink.

Pasta

Speedy Bolognese Bake

Makes 4 portions
Suitable for freezing

Bolognese is a family favourite, and this is my speedy version. It takes a little time to cook through, but you could cook the sauce in advance and bake the finished dish in just a few minutes.

✳ Heat the oil in a saucepan and fry the onion and red pepper for 2 minutes. Add the mince and cook until browned. Add the garlic and thyme and fry for 1 minute, then add the stock, tomatoes, sundried tomato paste and apple juice. Bring up to the boil, then simmer for 20 minutes.

✳ While the sauce is simmering, cook the pasta in a pan of boiling lightly salted water according to the packet instructions and preheat the grill.

✳ Add half the Parmesan to the sauce with the basil. Mix together and then tip in the pasta. Spoon this mixture into an ovenproof dish and sprinkle the top with the breadcrumbs and the remaining cheese. Grill for 5 minutes until lightly golden and crisp.

Ingredients

1 tbsp olive oil
1 red onion, finely chopped
50 g (2 oz) red pepper, deseeded and diced
225 g (8 oz) lean minced beef
1 garlic clove, crushed
1 tsp chopped fresh thyme
150 ml (5 fl oz) beef stock
1 x 400 g can chopped tomatoes
1½ tbsp sundried tomato paste
100 ml (3½ fl oz) apple juice
150 g (5 oz) fusilli
50 g (2 oz) Parmesan, grated
2 tbsp chopped fresh basil
20 g (¾ oz) fresh white breadcrumbs

Penne Pasta with Chicken

Makes 4 portions Suitable for freezing

Fresh pasta takes less time to cook than dried, but even if you use dried pasta this is still a speedy supper dish.

Ingredients

150 g (5 oz) fresh penne
1 tsp honey
1 boneless skinless chicken breast, sliced into strips
1 tbsp olive oil, for frying
50 g (2 oz) mushrooms, sliced
75 g (3 oz) roasted red pepper from a jar, finely chopped
2 tsp sundried tomato purée
1 tbsp snipped fresh chives
30 g (1 oz) mature Cheddar, grated

✳ Cook the pasta in a pan of boiling lightly salted water according to the packet instructions.

✳ Drizzle the honey over the chicken and season. Heat the oil in a frying pan and fry the chicken for 2–3 minutes until brown and cooked through. Add the mushrooms and fry for 30 seconds, then add all the remaining ingredients with the pasta and toss everything together over the heat. Season to taste.

Ham and Pea Pasta

Makes 4 portions

A tasty pasta dish that takes less than ten minutes to prepare from start to finish.

Ingredients

150 g (5 oz) fresh penne
50 g (2 oz) peas
75 g (3 oz) ham, diced
150 ml (5 fl oz) chicken stock
3 tbsp double cream
50 g (2 oz) mature Cheddar, grated

✳ Cook the pasta in a pan of boiling lightly salted water according to the packet instructions. About 4 minutes before the end of the cooking time, add the peas. Drain.

✳ Put the ham, stock and pasta in a pan and bring up to the boil. Add the cream and simmer for 3 minutes.

✳ Remove the pan from the heat, add the cheese and stir until the sauce has thickened slightly. Serve immediately.

Macaroni with Smoked Bacon and Courgette

Bacon and courgette make a delicious combination, and here they give macaroni a new partner instead of the classic cheese sauce!

Makes 6 portions Suitable for freezing

Ingredients

150 g (5 oz) macaroni
3 thick slices smoked bacon, diced
2 small courgettes, diced
1 tomato, deseeded and diced
2 tbsp snipped fresh chives
3 tbsp crème fraîche
50 g (2 oz) Parmesan, grated

★ Cook the pasta in a pan of boiling lightly salted water according to the packet instructions. Drain, reserving 150 ml (5 fl oz) of the cooking water.

★ While the pasta is cooking, dry-fry the bacon for 2 minutes in a frying pan. Add the courgettes and fry for 5 minutes until they are soft and lightly golden, then add the tomato and chives.

★ Add the pasta to the frying pan with the reserved water, crème fraîche and Parmesan. Toss together over the heat for 2 minutes. Season well, then serve.

Tomato and Basil Gnocchi

You can buy ready-made gnocchi in most supermarkets; it is perfect for a speedy supper as it takes only a couple of minutes to cook.

Makes 4 portions Suitable for freezing

Ingredients

1 x 500 g packet fresh gnocchi
1 tbsp olive oil
1 onion, chopped
1 garlic clove, crushed
1 x 400 g can chopped tomatoes
100 ml (3½ fl oz) vegetable stock
1 tsp sundried tomato paste
1 tbsp chopped fresh basil
½ ball mozzarella, cubed
30 g (1 oz) Parmesan, grated

★ Cook the gnocchi in a pan of boiling lightly salted water according to the packet instructions. Drain.

★ Heat the oil in a saucepan and fry the onion for 4 minutes, then add the garlic. Add the tomatoes, stock and tomato paste, bring up to the boil, then simmer for 5 minutes. Scatter over the basil, tip in the gnocchi, mix everything together and season.

★ Preheat the grill. Tip the mixture into a shallow dish and top with mozzarella and Parmesan. Cook under a hot grill for a few minutes until the cheese is bubbling.

Chicken, Broccoli, Pea and Tomato Pasta

Ingredients

150 g (5 oz) fusilli
50 g (2 oz) frozen peas
100 g (3½ oz) broccoli florets
1 tbsp olive oil
100 g (3½ oz) chicken
 breast, sliced
1 garlic clove, crushed
¼ red chilli, diced
200 ml (7 fl oz) chicken stock
1 tbsp cornflour
100 g (3½ oz) cherry
 tomatoes, quartered
50 g (2 oz) Parmesan, grated
2 tbsp chopped fresh basil

Boil the kettle

When using boiling water to cook, boil the kettle and pour the boiling water into a saucepan, so no need to wait for the pan to boil from cold.

This colourful dish looks as good as it tastes and it's super-healthy and super-quick too!

✴ Cook the pasta in a pan of boiling lightly salted water according to the packet instructions. About 4 minutes before the end of the cooking time, add the peas and broccoli. Drain.

✴ Heat the oil in a frying pan and fry the chicken until brown. Add the garlic and chilli and season. Pour in the stock. In a small bowl, mix the cornflour with 3 tablespoons of cold water and tip into the pan, stirring it in until the stock thickens.

✴ Add the pasta and vegetables to the chicken along with the tomatoes, Parmesan and basil. Toss everything together to heat through, then serve.

Roasted Red Pepper and Tomato Pasta

Makes 3 portions
Suitable for freezing

When you're rushing to get food on the table, take a short cut; use a jar of roasted red peppers and combine them with some tomato sauce.

★ Heat the oil in a saucepan and fry the onion for 5 minutes. Add the garlic and fry for 30 seconds, then add the peppers, tomatoes, tomato paste, balsamic vinegar and sugar and some seasoning. Bring up to the boil, cover and simmer for 5 minutes. Remove from the heat and allow to cool for a minute or so, then blend using a hand blender.

★ While you are making the sauce, cook the pasta in a pan of boiling lightly salted water according to the packet instructions. Drain, then tip the pasta into the sauce with the basil. Toss to coat then serve scattered with the basil leaves and Parmesan.

Ingredients

1 tbsp olive oil
1 onion, finely chopped
1 garlic clove, crushed or
    1 tsp garlic purée
75 g (3 oz) roasted skinned red
    peppers from a jar, chopped
1 x 400 g can chopped
    tomatoes
2 tsp sundried tomato paste
1 tsp balsamic vinegar
1 tsp caster sugar
175 g (6 oz) spaghetti
    or mafaldine
2 tbsp chopped fresh basil,
    plus a few whole leaves,
    to garnish
grated Parmesan, to serve

Tasty Chicken and Pasta Salad

Ingredients

150 g (5 oz) pasta
3 heaped tbsp chopped fresh
   basil, plus a few whole
   leaves, to garnish
100 g (3½ oz) cherry tomatoes,
   quartered
50 g (2 oz) canned sweetcorn,
   drained
125 g (4 oz) cooked chicken
   breast, diced

Dressing

1 tbsp rice wine vinegar
3 tbsp olive oil
1 tsp caster sugar
½ tsp Dijon mustard
1 tsp soy sauce

This tasty pasta salad is also great for lunchboxes and picnics.

✳ Cook the pasta in a pan of boiling lightly salted water according to the packet instructions. Drain and refresh in cold water.

✳ Measure all of the dressing ingredients into a mixing bowl. Whisk together and season. Mix the pasta with the remaining ingredients, season with salt and pepper and toss with the dressing. Scatter over the fresh basil leaves.

Easy lunchboxes

Use something from last night's dinner for your child's lunchbox, like a pasta salad or cold tortilla.

Prawns with Tomato and Mascarpone

Makes 6 portions

A lovely creamy tomato sauce with prawns.

✷ Cook the pasta in a pan of boiling lightly salted water according to the packet instructions. Drain.

✷ While the pasta is cooking, make the sauce. Heat the oil in a saucepan and fry the onion for 5 minutes. Add the garlic and fry for 30 seconds, then add the tomatoes, sugar and pesto. Season. Bring to the boil, then cover and simmer for 5 minutes.

✷ Remove from the heat, spoon in the mascarpone, and blend until smooth using an electric hand blender. Add the prawns and return to the heat, stirring until bubbling. Tip in the pasta and Parmesan, toss everything together and serve immediately.

Ingredients

175 g (6 oz) pasta shells
1 tbsp olive oil
1 onion, finely chopped
1 garlic clove, crushed
1 x 400 g can chopped
    tomatoes
1 tsp caster sugar
1 tbsp red pesto
3 tbsp mascarpone
175 g (6 oz) cooked large
    king prawns
30 g (1 oz) Parmesan, grated

Quick Pasta Sauces

These are ideal to use with leftover pasta – simply refresh it by pouring boiling water over it, or cook some fresh pasta, which will be ready in minutes.

* Mix 2 tbsp sundried tomato paste or pesto with 150 g (5 oz) cooked pasta, then your favourite ingredients, such as diced cooked chicken, some chopped vegetables, or perhaps cubes of mozzarella cheese.

* Heat 100 g (3½ oz) full-fat crème fraîche, then add 150 g (5 oz) penne and 30 g (1 oz) Parmesan. Toss everything together, perhaps adding other ingredients such as bacon, ham or broccoli.

* Mix 250 ml (8 fl oz) passata with 1 tbsp sundried tomato paste, 1 tsp fresh thyme leaves, 1 tbsp freshly grated Parmesan and a dash of sugar for a quick tomato sauce. Heat the sauce and combine with 150 g (5 oz) pasta, serving it with some freshly torn basil and chunks of mozzarella.

* Toss 150 g (5 oz) cooked pasta with 3 tbsp of your favourite salad dressing. Add other ingredients such as tomatoes, tuna, cooked chicken, peas and sweetcorn.

* Mix tuna, mayonnaise and sweetcorn together with leftover pasta for a cold pasta salad, or combine cooked pasta with Caesar dressing, chicken, avocado and tomato.

* Mix 200 ml (7 fl oz) passata with 2 tbsp crème fraîche, 1 tbsp red pesto and 1 tbsp fresh basil for a creamy tomato sauce.

* Mix 3 tbsp oil with 1 tbsp sweet balsamic vinegar, 1 tsp soy sauce and a dash of sugar for a quick cold dressing for pasta. Mix with diced cooked chicken, sweetcorn and halved cherry tomatoes.

Salami, Mozzarella and Tomato Pasta

Ingredients

150 g (5 oz) fusilli
50 g (2 oz) salami slices, roughly chopped
2 tbsp pesto
1 tsp balsamic vinegar
a handful of fresh basil leaves, chopped
150 g (5 oz) cherry tomatoes, halved
250 g (9 oz) mozzarella, diced

This speedy pasta dish needs very little preparation or cooking and is on the table in under 15 minutes.

✳ Cook the pasta in a pan of boiling lightly salted water according to the packet instructions. Drain.

✳ Dry-fry the salami in a frying pan for a few minutes until crisp, then add this to the pasta with the remaining ingredients. Mix everything together well, season and serve.

Cooking pasta

Cook more pasta than needed for a specific recipe, and while still warm, toss with a little oil to prevent sticking as it cools. Place the pasta in an open plastic container, when cool toss again, cover and store in the fridge. Use in pasta salads or reheat by putting into a pan of boiling water for approximately 1 minute.

Ingredients

1 tbsp olive oil
1 large onion, finely chopped
2 garlic cloves, crushed
2 x 400 g cans chopped
   tomatoes
2 tbsp tomato purée
2 tbsp red pesto
1 tsp sugar
1– 2 tsp balsamic vinegar
2 handfuls of fresh basil
   leaves, chopped
250 g (9 oz) spaghetti
grated Parmesan, to serve

Quick Tomato Sauce with Spaghetti

Adding red pesto to a tomato sauce gives it a great taste. You can leave out the basil if your little one doesn't like green bits.

✳ Heat the oil in a saucepan and cook the onion for 5 minutes. Add the garlic and fry for 1 minute. Add the tomatoes, tomato purée, pesto and sugar. Bring up to the boil, then simmer for 10 minutes, stirring from time to time. Remove from the heat, add the balsamic vinegar and blend until smooth using a hand blender, then stir in the basil.

✳ Meanwhile, cook the spaghetti in a pan of boiling lightly salted water according to the packet instructions, drain, then tip into the tomato sauce. Serve with Parmesan cheese scattered over.

Fish

Prawn Pilau

It's easy to make this using express rice, which takes just 2 minutes to cook in a microwave.

Ingredients

20 g (¾ oz) butter, for frying
1 onion, chopped
¼ red pepper, deseeded and finely diced
50 g (2 oz) frozen peas
50g (2 oz) mushrooms, sliced
1 garlic clove, crushed
150 g (5 oz) king prawns, shelled
250 g (9 oz) packet express long grain rice
1 tbsp soy sauce
1 tbsp sweet chilli sauce

✳ Melt the butter in a frying pan, and fry the onion and pepper for 4 minutes.

✳ Meanwhile, cook the peas in a pan of boiling water for 4 minutes. Drain.

✳ Add the mushrooms and garlic to the onions, fry for 1 minute, then add the prawns and peas.

✳ Cook the rice in a microwave for 2 minutes or according to the packet instructions. Add the rice to the pan with the soy sauce and sweet chilli sauce. Toss together and season.

Quick Tuna, Broccoli and Tomato Pasta

A can of tuna is a brilliant storecupboard standby, and combined with quick-cooking pasta and superhealthy broccoli makes a speedy, nutritious and tasty meal.

Ingredients

Makes 1 portion

30 g (1 oz) baby pasta shells
30 g (1 oz) broccoli florets, chopped
3 tbsp passata
1 tbsp sundried tomato paste
½ x 185 g can tuna in sunflower oil
1 tsp chopped fresh basil
1 tbsp grated Parmesan

✳ Cook the pasta in a pan of lightly salted boiling water according to the packet instructions. About 3 minutes before the end of the cooking time, add the broccoli.

✳ Drain the pasta and broccoli and return them to the pan. Add the remaining ingredients to the pasta, stir well to combine and serve immediately.

Tuna Pasta Bake

Ingredients

150 g (5 oz) penne
1 small head of broccoli,
  broken into bite-sized florets
1 x 400 g can chopped
  tomatoes
1 tbsp tomato purée
1 tbsp brown sugar
200 ml (7 fl oz) vegetable
  stock
olive oil, for frying
1 large courgette, chopped
2 red, yellow or orange
  peppers, deseeded and
  chopped
½ onion, sliced
1 garlic clove, crushed
1 x 185 g can of tuna, drained
200 g (7 oz) Gruyère, grated

★ Preheat the oven to 200°C/180°C Fan/400°F/Gas 6.

★ Cook the pasta in a pan of boiling salted water according to the packet instructions.

★ About 5 minutes before the end of the cooking time, add the broccoli. Drain.

★ Meanwhile, in a saucepan, simmer the tomatoes and purée with the brown sugar and stock.

★ In a large pan, heat a little olive oil and soften the courgette, peppers, onion and garlic.

★ Tip the tomato mixture into the softened vegetable mixture.

★ Combine the sauce, drained pasta and broccoli and tuna, place in an ovenproof dish and cover with the cheese. Bake in the oven for 8 minutes or until the cheese has melted.

Cod and Salmon Fishcakes

Makes 6 portions
Suitable for freezing

The sweet chilli sauce and grated Cheddar add a delicious flavour to these fishcakes. You could also make them using just salmon.

∗ Measure all the ingredients, except the oil, into a food processor and whiz until combined. Divide up the mixture and shape it into 6 fishcakes.

∗ Heat the oil in a frying pan. Fry the fishcakes for 6–8 minutes, turning them halfway through cooking so both sides are golden and the fishcakes are cooked through. Blot on kitchen paper and allow to cool slightly before serving.

Ingredients

125 g (4 oz) skinless salmon fillet, cut into cubes
125 g (4 oz) skinless cod fillet, cut into cubes
6 spring onions, chopped
100 g (3½ oz) fresh breadcrumbs
1 tbsp soy sauce
2 tsp sweet chilli sauce
1 egg yolk
50 g (2 oz) Cheddar, grated
a little sunflower oil, for frying

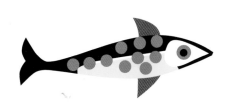

Salmon and Broccoli Pasta Bake

Ingredients

150 g (5 oz) fusilli
75 g (3 oz) broccoli florets
30 g (1 oz) butter
1 leek, chopped
3 tbsp plain flour
450 ml (16 fl oz) milk
75 g (3 oz) fresh Parmesan, grated
150 g (5 oz) skinless salmon fillet
juice of ½ lemon
30 g (1 oz) Cheddar, grated
1 tomato, deseeded and diced

When cooking pasta, save time and washing up by adding the vegetables to the same pan and letting them cook along with the pasta for the last few minutes.

★ Cook the pasta in a pan of boiling salted water according to the packet instructions. About 3 minutes before the end of the cooking time add the broccoli. Drain.

★ While the pasta is cooking, melt the butter in a saucepan. Add the leek and stir until softened. Add the flour, then blend in the milk, stir until thickened and smooth. Add the Parmesan and season.

★ Put the salmon in a microwaveable dish and sprinkle with the lemon juice. Cover the dish with cling film and poke holes in it. Cook in the microwave for approximately 2 minutes on full power. Flake the cooked fish into the sauce and add the pasta, broccoli and cooking liquid from the fish. Mix and spoon into a shallow dish, then sprinkle with the Cheddar and tomato. Put under a hot grill for 5 minutes until bubbling.

Orange and Soy Sole

Ingredients

2 lemon sole fillets, skinned
plain flour, for dusting
a knob of butter, for frying
1 tbsp orange juice
1 tsp soy sauce

★ Season the fish fillets and coat them on both sides with the flour, shaking off any excess.

★ Melt the butter in a frying pan until foaming, add the fish fillets and fry for 1½ minutes. Turn them over and then fry for 1 minute more.

★ Mix the orange juice and soy sauce together, pour it over the fish and let the sauce bubble away for 30 seconds.

★ Serve immediately.

Prawn and Noodle Laksa

Ingredients

100 g (3½ oz) medium egg noodles
1 tbsp sunflower oil
1 onion, finely chopped
½ red chilli, finely diced
1 garlic clove, crushed
1 tsp grated fresh root ginger
1 tbsp curry paste
400 ml (14 fl oz) coconut milk
300 ml (½ pint) chicken stock
2 tsp soy sauce
1 tsp fish sauce
1 tbsp brown sugar
zest and juice of ½ large lime
100 g (3½ oz) broccoli florets
150 g (5 oz) raw prawns, shelled

★ Cook the noodles in a pan of boiling water according to the packet instructions. Drain.

★ Heat the oil in a saucepan and fry the onion for 5 minutes, then add the chilli, garlic and ginger. Add the curry paste, then blend in the coconut milk, stock, soy and fish sauces, sugar and lime zest and juice. Add the broccoli and prawns and simmer for 3 minutes until the prawns have turned pink.

★ Divide the noodles between 4 bowls and spoon in the laksa.

Teriyaki Salmon Kebabs

Ingredients

2 tbsp brown sugar
2 tbsp soy sauce
2 tbsp rice wine vinegar
1 tsp sesame oil
250 g (9 oz) skinless
    salmon fillet
1 courgette, sliced into
    1-cm (½-in) slices
a little oil, for roasting
6 wooden skewers

Oily fish like salmon and trout are full of omega 3 essential fatty acids, which boost brain power.

✳ Preheat the oven to 220°C/200°C Fan/425°F/Gas 7.

✳ Combine the sugar, soy sauce, rice vinegar and sesame oil in a bowl.

✳ Cut the salmon into cubes and coat them and the courgette in the teriyaki marinade. Leave to marinate for 10 minutes, or longer if possible.

✳ Thread the salmon and courgette slices onto the skewers, alternating them as you go, and reserve the marinade. Place the kebabs onto a baking sheet, drizzle over a little oil and roast in the oven for 12–15 minutes or until the salmon is cooked through. While the salmon is cooking, boil the marinade until reduced and thickened.

✳ Place the kebabs on a plate and pour over the sauce. Serve with quick-cook rice or noodles if you like.

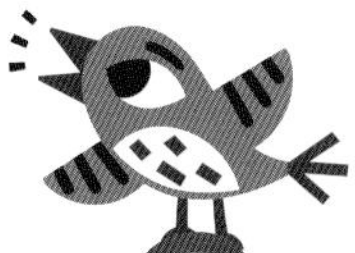

Prawn Curry

Makes 4 portions
Suitable for freezing

Succulent prawns in a delicious fruity curried sauce will satisfy any starving child. Serve the curry on a bed of rice with a few poppadoms on the side if they're really ravenous!

✶ Heat the oil in a saucepan, then add the onion and pepper and fry for 5 minutes. Add the ginger and garam masala, then the chopped tomatoes, stock, coconut, mango chutney and tomato purée. Bring to the boil, season, then cover with a lid and simmer for 10–15 minutes.

✶ Add the prawns and cook, stirring, until they have turned pink. Serve with quick-cook rice.

Ingredients

2 tbsp oil
1 onion, diced
1 red pepper, deseeded and finely diced
1 tsp grated fresh root ginger
1 tbsp garam masala
1 x 400 g can chopped tomatoes
300 ml (½ pint) chicken stock
75 g (3 oz) creamed coconut
2 tsp mango chutney
1 tbsp tomato purée
350 g (12 oz) raw king prawns

Makes 4 portions

Fresh Haddock Kedgeree

Ingredients

250 g (9 oz) fresh haddock
   fillets
juice of ½ lemon
200 g (7 oz) basmati rice
100 g (3½ oz) frozen peas
30 g (1 oz) butter
2 onions, finely diced
1 tsp grated fresh root ginger
50 g (2 oz) mushrooms,
   chopped
½ tsp garam masala
¼ tsp turmeric
½ tsp korma curry paste
1 tsp lemon juice
1 tbsp mango chutney
lemon wedges, to serve
   (optional)

There are lots of reasons why you should add fish to your toddler's plate; it's high in protein, low in saturated fat and a good source of vitamin D and many B vitamins.

★ Put the haddock in a suitable microwaveable dish and sprinkle with the lemon juice. Cover the dish with cling film and poke holes in it. Cook in the microwave on high for approximately 2 minutes or until the fish flakes easily with a fork. Flake the cooked fish into large pieces.

★ Cook the rice in a pan of boiling water according to the packet instructions, and about 5 minutes before the end of the cooking time, add the peas. Drain.

★ Melt the butter in a frying pan and fry the onions for 5 minutes, then add the ginger and mushrooms and fry for 2 minutes more. Stir in the spices, then tip in the rice and peas, lemon juice and mango chutney. Season well. Finally, add the cooked fish, toss together without breaking up the fish flakes too much, then serve with lemon wedges, if using.

Prawn Stir-Fry in a Sweet and Sour Sauce

Makes 4 portions
Suitable for freezing

Prawns are a good source of protein, omega 3 fatty acids, iron, zinc and vitamin E. Although prawns have a high cholesterol content, they are low in saturated fat, which is the fat that raises cholesterol levels.

✳ Heat the oil in a large frying pan or wok. Add the vegetables and stir-fry for 3–4 minutes until they are nearly cooked. Add the prawns and ginger and fry for 1 minute.

✳ Meanwhile, whisk all of the sauce ingredients together in a bowl until smooth. Add the sauce to the pan with the water chestnuts, bring to the boil, then stir until thickened and the prawns have turned pink. Season to taste, then serve with rice.

Ingredients

2 tbsp olive oil
1 onion, sliced
100 g (3½ oz) broccoli florets
½ red pepper, thinly sliced
175 g (6 oz) baby corn, thinly sliced
250 g (9 oz) raw large king prawns
½ tsp grated fresh root ginger
150 g (5 oz) water chestnuts, sliced in half

Sweet and sour sauce

4 tbsp tomato ketchup
1½ tbsp rice wine vinegar
1½ tsp brown sugar
1½–2 tbsp soy sauce
200 ml (7 fl oz) water
1 tbsp cornflour

Frozen vegetables

Frozen vegetables are just as nutritious as fresh, as they are frozen within hours of picking which locks in all the nutrients.

Lemon Sole Goujons

Ingredients

450 g (1 lb) skinless lemon
   sole fillets (approx. 4 fillets)
a little plain flour, for dusting
2 eggs, beaten
50 g (2 oz) Japanese
   breadcrumbs
30 g (1 oz) Parmesan, grated
2 tbsp snipped chives
zest of ½ lemon
a little oil and butter, for frying

Try coating fish in Japanese (Panko) breadcrumbs instead of ordinary breadcrumbs – they have a lovely light texture. You can buy Panko breadcrumbs in oriental food stores or most large supermarkets. If you prefer, you could use the same quantity of crushed cornflakes to coat the fish instead.

✶ Slice each fillet into thin strips – you should get about 4 strips from each fillet. Put the flour onto a plate and the eggs into a shallow bowl. Season the strips, toss them in the flour, then dip the sole into the beaten egg.

✶ Mix the breadcrumbs, Parmesan, chives and lemon zest together on a plate. Roll each fish strip in the mixture to coat them on all sides.

✶ Heat the oil and butter in a frying pan and fry the goujons for a few minutes on each side until lightly golden and crisp.

Keeping salt

To keep salt from clogging
in the shaker, add half a
teaspoon of uncooked rice.

Poultry

Chicken and Sweetcorn Chowder

This soup is a meal in itself and makes a satisfying lunch or supper. Serve with a salad on the side or warm hunks of crusty bread for mopping up the last delicious bits of chowder.

Ingredients

30 g (1 oz) butter
1 onion, finely chopped
2 medium carrots, finely diced
30 g (1 oz) plain flour
600 ml (1 pint) chicken stock
50 g (2 oz) frozen peas
50 g (2 oz) canned sweetcorn, drained
100 g (3½ oz) cooked chicken, finely diced
3 tbsp double cream

✶ Melt the butter in a saucepan, then add the onion and carrots and fry for 5 minutes until soft. Sprinkle over the flour then blend in the stock. Bring to the boil, cover with a lid and leave to simmer for 10 minutes.

✶ Add the peas after 5 minutes, then add the sweetcorn, chicken and cream. Stir to combine then season with salt and pepper.

Thai Noodle Soup

A speedy soup for lunch, but if you prefer to prepare it ahead and eat it later, make the soup and add the noodles when you reheat it.

Ingredients

1 tbsp olive oil
2 small onions, finely chopped
½ red chilli, diced
1 garlic clove, crushed
1½ tsp korma curry paste
1 boneless, skinless chicken breast, thinly sliced
1 x 400 ml can coconut milk
450 ml (16 fl oz) chicken stock
100 g (3½ oz) broccoli florets
1 tsp sweet chilli sauce
½ tsp fish sauce
50 g (2 oz) vermicelli rice noodles

✶ Heat the oil in a saucepan or wok, then add the onions, chilli and garlic and sauté for 3–4 minutes. Add the korma paste, then the chicken and fry for 1 minute. Pour in the coconut milk and stock and bring to the boil. Add the broccoli, chilli sauce and fish sauce, then simmer for 3–4 minutes until the chicken and broccoli are cooked.

✶ Pour boiling water over the noodles and leave them for 2–3 minutes. Drain the noodles and add them to the soup. Serve at once.

Creamy Chicken and Vegetable Soup

Ingredients

30 g (1 oz) butter
1 large onion, finely chopped
100 g (3½ oz) carrots, diced
1 stick celery, diced
30 g (1 oz) plain flour
1 litre (1¾ pints) chicken stock
50 g (2 oz) small pasta shells
75 g (3 oz) cooked chicken
   breast, diced
3 tbsp double cream
1 tbsp snipped fresh chives

My children all love this soup – so simple, but quite delicious.

✳ Heat the butter in a saucepan, and fry the onion for
2 minutes. Add the carrots and celery and fry for 5 minutes.
Stir in the flour, blend in the stock, then bring the soup
to the boil. Cover and simmer for 10 minutes until the
vegetables are tender.

✳ Meanwhile, cook the pasta in a pan of boiling lightly
salted water according to the packet instructions. Drain.

✳ Add the diced chicken, double cream, pasta and
chives to the soup and simmer all together for 3 minutes.
Season to taste.

Chicken, Pesto and Tomato Pasta

A quick, virtually no-cook pasta sauce which is colourful and tasty.

Makes 1 portion

Ingredients

30 g (1 oz) baby pasta shells
1 tbsp pesto
20 g (¾ oz) cooked chicken, diced
1 tbsp chopped fresh basil
1 small tomato, finely chopped
2 tbsp grated Parmesan

✳ Cook the pasta in a pan of lightly salted boiling water according to the packet instructions. Drain and return to the pan.

✳ Add the remaining ingredients to the pan and mix well. Cook for a minute or two to heat everything through, and serve.

Chicken and Rice Salad

Makes 4 portions

Pre-cooked rice is perfect for whipping up this delicious salad, but if you don't have any, use express rice that cooks in just 10 minutes.

Ingredients

1 x 250 g packet Uncle Ben's Express rice
1 cooked chicken breast, diced
4 tbsp canned sweetcorn, drained
6 spring onions, sliced
100 g (3½ oz) cherry tomatoes, quartered
2 tbsp chopped fresh basil

Dressing

4 tbsp olive oil
1 tbsp soy sauce
1 tbsp sweet balsamic vinegar
1½ tsp caster sugar

✳ Cook the rice in the microwave according to the packet instructions – it usually takes 2 minutes.

✳ Mix all the dressing ingredients together in a large bowl. Add the cooked rice and all the remaining ingredients, and mix well to combine. Season and serve immediately.

Chicken Parmigiana

Makes 4 portions
Suitable for freezing

This classic Italian dish makes a tasty meal for the whole family. Usually it takes a little time to prepare, but this is my super-quick recipe with all the flavour of the original.

✳ Preheat the grill until hot. Slice the chicken in half through the middle, lay the two halves on a chopping board, cover them with a piece of cling film, then bash them using a rolling pin so you have 4 thin slices.

✳ Put the egg in a shallow bowl, and on a plate mix the breadcrumbs and Parmesan together. Dip the chicken in the egg then coat it in the breadcrumbs, making sure it is covered on all sides. Place the coated chicken on a baking sheet and grill for about 4 minutes on each side until cooked through.

✳ Meanwhile, warm the tomato sauce in the microwave and pour it into a shallow baking dish. Put the chicken in the dish, then scatter over the cheese and basil. Place the chicken back under the grill for a few minutes until the cheese is bubbling and lightly golden brown. Serve with salad or garlic bread.

Ingredients

2 boneless, skinless
  chicken breasts
2 eggs, beaten
50 g (2 oz) white breadcrumbs
50 g (2 oz) Parmesan, grated
1 x 300 g tub good-quality
  ready-made tomato sauce
250 g (9 oz) mozzarella, sliced
2 tbsp chopped fresh basil

Mini Chicken Burgers

Makes 8 burgers
Suitable for freezing before cooking

Chicken makes a nice change from minced beef, but you can make this with red meat too.

* Mix all of the burger ingredients together in a bowl. Season and shape into 8 burgers.

* Preheat the grill. Arrange the burgers on a baking sheet and put a little butter, margarine or Marmite on top of each one. Cook under a hot grill for about 5 minutes on each side until cooked through.

* Alternatively, you can fry them. Heat the oil in a frying pan and cook the burgers for 5–6 minutes, turning halfway through, until lightly golden and cooked through in the middle.

* Serve the burgers on their own or with mini buns or bagels and a little mayonnaise or ketchup and salad.

Ingredients

250 g (9 oz) minced chicken or turkey
5 spring onions, chopped
1 tbsp chopped fresh thyme
½ apple, grated
50 g (2 oz) Parmesan, grated
50 g (2 oz) carrot, grated
50 g (2 oz) fresh white breadcrumbs
1 tbsp sweet chilli sauce
2 tsp soy sauce

a little butter, margarine or Marmite to grill (optional)
a little oil, for frying (optional)

Chicken and Vegetable Stir-Fry

Ingredients

2 tbsp olive oil, plus a little
  extra for frying
2 boneless, skinless chicken
  breasts, sliced into strips
1 tbsp honey
1 red onion, sliced
1 garlic clove, crushed
1 red pepper, deseeded
  and sliced
1 yellow pepper,
  deseeded and sliced
1 courgette, sliced into batons
250 g (9 oz) brown
  mushrooms, thickly sliced
1 tbsp oyster sauce
1 tbsp soy sauce
1 tsp hoisin sauce

One of my favourite chicken stir-fries – serve with
noodles or rice.

✳ Heat 1 tablespoon of the oil in a frying pan or wok.
Toss the chicken in the honey and season, then stir-fry
over a high heat for 3–4 minutes until golden and
cooked through. Transfer to a plate.

✳ Heat the remaining oil in the frying pan or wok,
add the onion and fry for 3–4 minutes. Add the garlic,
peppers and courgette and fry for 3 minutes, then
add the cooked chicken.

✳ Heat a little oil in another frying pan and fry the
mushrooms for 3 minutes until just cooked. Add these to
the other vegetables along with the oyster, soy and hoisin
sauces and season to taste. Toss together and heat through.

Honey Chicken Wraps

Makes 4 wraps

Ingredients

2 boneless, skinless chicken breasts,
   sliced into strips
1 tbsp each soy sauce, lemon juice and honey
1 tbsp oil
4 tortilla wraps
a little light mayonnaise
2 tomatoes, deseeded and sliced
¼ cucumber, sliced into thin batons
iceberg lettuce, shredded
50 g (2 oz) Cheddar, grated

✴ Put the chicken into a bowl, pour over the soy sauce, lemon juice and honey and leave to marinate for as long as possible.

✴ Remove the chicken from the marinade using a slotted spoon. Heat the oil in a frying pan and fry the chicken for 3–4 minutes until golden and cooked through.

✴ Warm the wraps for 1 minute in the microwave and set aside on a plate. Spread the mayonnaise along one end of a wrap, top with tomatoes, cucumber and lettuce, then spoon over the chicken and sprinkle with the cheese. Roll up around the filling, tucking in the sides so the wrap is sealed at both ends. Cut the wrap in half diagonally. Repeat with the remaining ingredients.

Hot Plum Chicken Wraps

Makes 4 wraps

The sweet and sour flavours in plum sauce add a little richness to these chicken wraps.

Ingredients

2 boneless, skinless chicken breasts,
   sliced into strips
1 tbsp plum sauce, plus 4 tbsp for the wraps
2 tsp soy sauce
a little oil, for frying
4 tortilla wraps
4 tbsp light mayonnaise
¼ cucumber, sliced into thin strips
4 spring onions, sliced into thin strips
iceberg lettuce, shredded

✴ Put the chicken into a bowl and pour over the plum and soy sauces. Heat a little oil in a frying pan and fry the chicken for 3–4 minutes until golden brown and cooked through.

✴ Warm the wraps for 1 minute in the microwave and set aside on a plate. Spread 1 tablespoon each of mayonnaise and plum sauce along one end of a wrap, then top with cucumber, spring onions, shredded lettuce and some chicken. Roll up around the filling, tucking in the sides so the wrap is sealed at both ends. Cut the wrap in half diagonally. Repeat with the remaining ingredients until all 4 wraps are made.

Chicken Wrap with Sweetcorn and Cucumber

Makes 2 wraps

Wraps make a delicious and simple meal, perfect for children of any age. Children love getting involved in making these, but they might need help rolling them – wrap the bases in foil if they aren't quite sealed!

Ingredients

2 mini tortilla wraps
2 tbsp light mayonnaise
1 tsp lemon juice
½ cooked chicken breast, diced
2 tbsp canned sweetcorn, drained
50 g (2 oz) cucumber, diced
2 spring onions, sliced
1 tbsp chopped fresh basil

✶ Warm the wraps for 1 minute in the microwave then set them aside on a board.

✶ Mix the remaining ingredients together in a bowl. Divide the mixture into two, arranging the filling at one end of each wrap then rolling up around it, tucking in the sides so the wrap is sealed at both ends. Cut the wrap in half diagonally and serve.

Chicken Salad Wrap

Ingredients

2 mini tortilla wraps
2 tbsp light mayonnaise
a few drops Worcestershire sauce
2 lettuce leaves, sliced
½ cooked chicken breast, sliced
1 tomato, deseeded and sliced
2 tbsp grated Parmesan

Makes 2 wraps

✶ Warm the wraps in the microwave for 1 minute then set them aside on a board.

✶ Mix the mayonnaise and Worcestershire sauce together and spread this over the wraps. Put the lettuce, chicken, tomato and cheese at one end of each wrap then roll up around it, tucking in the sides so the wrap is sealed at both ends. Cut the wrap in half diagonally and serve.

Keep sharp

Don't forget to sharpen your knives, it takes much longer to chop with a blunt knife.

Chicken Chow Mein

Ingredients

100 g (3½ oz) medium
    egg noodles
1 boneless, skinless chicken
    breast, thinly sliced
1 tbsp hoisin sauce
1 tbsp olive oil
1 red pepper, deseeded
    and thinly sliced
1 bunch spring onions, sliced
200 g (7 oz) beansprouts

Sauce

½ tsp grated root ginger
1 garlic clove, crushed
1 tbsp tomato ketchup
1 tbsp oyster sauce
1 tbsp soy sauce

I don't cook the beansprouts in this dish as I like them
to remain crunchy, and they cook down a little just from
the heat of the noodles.

✳ Cook the noodles in a pan of boiling salted water
according to the packet instructions. Drain.

✳ Toss the chicken in the hoisin sauce. Heat the oil in
a frying pan and brown the chicken. Add the pepper and
spring onions and fry for 2 minutes with the chicken.

✳ Combine all the sauce ingredients, and pour into
the pan along with 3 tablespoons of cold water. Add
the noodles and toss everything together. Turn the heat
off and stir through the beansprouts. Serve at once.

Garlic and ginger
To save time use garlic
purée or ginger purée
instead of fresh.

Sticky Chicken Strips

All your family will love these tasty chicken strips – they are very moreish, you might even need to make double!

Makes 3 portions
Suitable for freezing

Ingredients

2 tbsp tomato ketchup
1 tbsp soy sauce
1 tbsp lemon juice
½ tsp Worcestershire sauce
2 tsp brown sugar
2 tsp tomato purée
2 boneless, skinless chicken breasts, sliced into strips
1 tbsp olive oil

∗ Combine the first 6 ingredients in a small bowl and toss the chicken strips in 1 tablespoon of this sauce.

∗ Heat the oil in a frying pan, then season and fry the chicken until brown and just cooked through – this will take 4–5 minutes. Add the remaining sauce and toss the chicken over the heat until it is glazed and sticky.

Italian Chicken

This quick and flexible dish can be served with rice, pasta or mash.

Makes 1 portion
Suitable for freezing

Ingredients

1 boneless, skinless chicken breast, sliced into strips
2 tbsp olive oil
½ red onion, chopped
½ tsp garlic purée
200 ml (7 fl oz) passata
100 ml (3½ fl oz) chicken stock
1 tsp tomato purée
pinch of sugar
1 tbsp chopped fresh basil

∗ Season the chicken. Heat half the oil in a frying pan and fry the chicken until sealed. Transfer to a plate.

∗ Heat the remaining oil in the same pan and fry the onion for 4 minutes, then add the garlic and fry for 30 seconds. Add the passata, stock, tomato purée and sugar and allow the mixture to bubble away for 2–3 minutes until slightly reduced. Return the chicken to the pan and heat it through. Stir in the basil and serve immediately.

Oriental Chicken Kebabs

Ingredients

400 g (14 oz) boneless chicken
  thigh or breast
1 courgette, sliced into 1-cm
  (½-in) slices
a little oil, for frying
6 wooden skewers

Marinade

3 tbsp sake
3 tbsp soy sauce
3 tbsp mirin
1 tbsp brown sugar

I like to brown the chicken first in a frying pan and then finish it off in the oven. You can make these skewers using chicken breasts or, just as delicious but less expensive, boned thighs. Serve the kebabs with quick-cook rice.

✳ Mix together the ingredients for the marinade in a bowl. Cut the chicken into cubes and add it to the marinade along with the courgettes. Leave to marinate for 5 minutes or as long as possible. Preheat the oven to 220°C/200°C Fan/425°F/Gas 7.

✳ Thread the chicken and courgette slices onto the skewers, alternating them as you go. Reserve the marinade. Heat the oil in a frying pan and quickly brown the skewers on both sides. Place the skewers on a baking sheet and roast them in the oven for 8–10 minutes until cooked through. If you are short of time leave the skewers in the frying pan and fry until cooked through.

✳ While the chicken is cooking, boil the marinade in a pan until reduced and thickened. Place the cooked chicken skewers on a plate and pour over the sauce to serve.

Griddled Chicken with Tomato and Cucumber Salsa

Makes 4 portions

My children love griddled chicken – it's a delicious, healthy way of cooking, requiring little fat to produce tender and succulent meat.

✳ Slice the chicken breasts in half through the middle. Lay the two halves on a chopping board and cover them with cling film. Using a rolling pin, bash the chicken to make 4 thin slices. Place the chicken in a shallow bowl and pour over the soy sauce, honey, oil and oregano. Season and leave to marinate for as long as you can, at least 10 minutes.

✳ Meanwhile, mix all of the salsa ingredients together in a small bowl. This salsa can be prepared ahead of time and kept in the fridge.

✳ Heat the sunflower oil in a frying pan until hot, then fry the chicken breasts for 2–3 minutes on each side until cooked through. Serve the chicken with the salsa. You can also griddle the chicken. Heat the griddle until hot and then cook the chicken for about 2 minutes on each side.

Ingredients

2 boneless, skinless
    chicken breasts
    (approx. 100 g/3½ oz)
2 tbsp soy sauce
1½ tbsp honey
1 tbsp olive oil
1 tsp dried oregano
1½ tbsp sunflower oil,
    for frying

Salsa

1 tomato, deseeded and diced
6-cm (2½-in) length of
    cucumber, diced
1 tbsp chopped fresh basil
1 tbsp olive oil
2 tsp rice wine vinegar

Ingredients

175 g (6 oz) long grain rice
1 carrot, diced
100 g (3½ oz) green beans,
   chopped
2 tbsp olive oil
1 large onion, chopped
1 large boneless, skinless
   chicken breast, diced
2 garlic cloves, crushed
4 spring onions, sliced
1½ tbsp soy sauce
1 tbsp sweet chilli sauce

Chicken and Veggie Fried Rice

This is a quick and nutritious dish, but for an even speedier supper use quick-cook rice.

✳ Bring a pan of water to the boil and cook the rice according to the packet instructions, along with the carrot. About 3 minutes before the end of the cooking time, add the beans. Drain.

✳ Heat the oil in a frying pan and cook the onion for 5 minutes until soft. Add the chicken and garlic and fry until lightly browned. Stir through the spring onions, then the rice and vegetables. Pour in the soy and sweet chilli sauce, toss everything together over the heat, season and serve immediately.

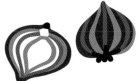

Nasi Goreng with Chicken and Prawns

Makes 4 portions
Suitable for freezing

An easy rice dish that's got loads of flavour. There are many different variations to nasi goreng, which is probably the best-known national recipe in Indonesia.

✳ Cook the rice in a pan of boiling salted water according to the packet instructions. To save time, use quick-cook rice. About 4 minutes before the end of the cooking time, add the peas. Drain.

✳ Heat the oil in a frying pan and cook the onion, red pepper and chilli for 5 minutes. Add the garlic, spring onions and chicken. Fry over the heat until the chicken is just cooked. Add the curry paste and caster sugar, then the rice and peas. Toss over the heat. Stir in the soy sauce and prawns and heat through.

✳ Meanwhile, in a bowl, beat the eggs with the milk and season. Melt the butter in a small frying pan or saucepan, tip in the egg mixture and stir over the heat until scrambled. Stir this through the rice and serve immediately.

Ingredients

175 g (6 oz) long grain rice
   (use quick-cook rice
   for speed)
75 g (3 oz) peas
2 tbsp olive oil
1 onion, finely chopped
½ red pepper, deseeded
   and diced
¼ red chilli, deseeded
   and chopped
2 garlic cloves, crushed
6 spring onions, sliced
1 boneless, skinless chicken
   breast, diced
1 tsp curry paste
1½ tsp caster sugar
1½ tbsp soy sauce
100 g (3½ oz) small cooked
   prawns
2 eggs
3 tbsp milk
a knob of butter, for frying

Chinese Chicken and Rice

Ingredients

175 g (6 oz) long grain rice
50 g (2 oz) frozen peas
1 tbsp olive oil, for frying
140 g (4½ oz) onion,
  finely chopped
75 g (3 oz) red pepper,
  deseeded and diced
1 tsp garlic purée
150 g (5 oz) chicken
  breast, diced
50 g (2 oz) canned
  sweetcorn, drained
2 eggs, lightly beaten
a little salt
1½ tsp sunflower oil, for frying

Sauce

2 tsp hoisin sauce
1 tsp ketchup
2 tsp soy sauce
1 tsp honey
100 ml (3½ fl oz) chicken stock

This is a family favourite in my house. If time is really tight, use quick-cook long grain rice.

✷ Cook the rice in a pan of boiling water according to the packet instructions. About 4 minutes before the end of the cooking time, add the peas. Drain well.

✷ Heat the oil in a frying pan and cook the onion for 3 minutes. Add the pepper and garlic purée and fry for 5 minutes until soft, then add the chicken and fry until just cooked. Tip in the rice, peas and sweetcorn and stir through.

✷ Meanwhile, mix all of the sauce ingredients together, then pour them over the rice and cook everything together for 1 minute.

✷ Season the eggs with a little salt and heat the oil in a frying pan. Make a thin omelette by pouring the eggs into the pan and swirling them around the base, then cook for 2–3 minutes until just set. Turn the omelette out onto a board and cut it into thin strips. Add the strips of egg to the rice and serve.

Chicken, Pepper and Broccoli Pasta

Ingredients

Makes 4 portions

200 g (7 oz) fusilli
100 g (3½ oz) broccoli florets
1 tbsp olive oil
2 onions, thinly sliced
2 garlic cloves, crushed
½ red pepper, deseeded and sliced
1 tbsp runny honey
1 large skinless chicken breast, sliced into strips
300 ml (½ pint) chicken stock
1 tbsp cornflour
30 g (1 oz) Parmesan, grated

✳ Cook the pasta in a pan of boiling lightly salted water according to the packet instructions. About 4 minutes before the end of the cooking time, add the broccoli. Drain.

✳ Heat the oil in a frying pan and fry the onions for 5 minutes. Add the garlic and fry for 2 minutes, then the pepper and fry for 2 minutes. Mix the honey with the chicken, add to the pan, cooking until sealed and lightly browned. Pour in the stock. In a bowl, blend the cornflour with 3 tbsp cold water. Add to the stock, bring to the boil, and cook, stirring, until thickened.

✳ Add the pasta and broccoli and heat through for a minute or two. Divide between bowls, scatter with the Parmesan, season and serve.

Smoked Chicken Tagliatelle

Smoked chicken has a fragrant flavour that many children love, and this recipe makes a sophisticated supper for children and adults alike.

Ingredients

Makes 4 portions

175 g (6 oz) fresh tagliatelle
4 tbsp olive oil
200 g (7 oz) cherry tomatoes, halved
1 boneless, skinless smoked chicken breast, shredded
30 g (1 oz) rocket, chopped
1½ tsp balsamic vinegar
50 g (2 oz) Parmesan, grated

✳ Cook the pasta in a pan of boiling lightly salted water according to the packet instructions. Drain, reserving 3 tablespoons of the cooking water.

✳ Warm the oil in a saucepan and add the tomatoes, chicken, rocket and balsamic vinegar. Toss in the pasta and mix together. Mix in the reserved pasta cooking water and the Parmesan, then season to taste. Serve warm.

Turkey Meatballs

Makes 5 portions
Suitable for freezing before cooking

This recipe makes 5 portions, but if that's too many, simply freeze the ones you don't need, by placing the uncooked meatballs on a tray lined with cling film, cover with more cling film and freeze. Once frozen, transfer them to a plastic freezer box. When you want them, simply defrost and cook.

✳ Put the pieces of bread into a bowl and pour over the milk. Leave to soak for 5 minutes, then mash with a fork. Add all the remaining ingredients, except the flour and oil, season and mix together.

✳ Shape the mixture into 25 small balls using your hands. Spread the plain flour over a plate and gently roll the meatballs in the flour so they are evenly coated.

✳ Heat the oil in a large frying pan and gently fry the meatballs for about 8 minutes until golden brown on the outside and cooked through in the middle. Serve with mashed potato and vegetables.

Ingredients

50 g (2 oz) white bread, torn into pieces
6 tbsp milk
300 g (11 oz) minced turkey
4 spring onions, sliced
3 tbsp canned sweetcorn, drained and roughly chopped
50 g (2 oz) Parmesan, grated
1 tsp chopped fresh thyme (optional)
plain flour, for dusting
3 tbsp olive oil, for frying

Mango and Apricot Chicken

Makes 3 portions

This is good served with rice. You can use express rice, which only takes 2 minutes to cook in a microwave.

✳ Toss the chicken in the honey and season. Heat the oil in a frying pan and fry the chicken quickly until brown and just cooked through. Set aside.

✳ Put all of the sauce ingredients plus 2 tablespoons of water into the pan. Bring to the boil, return the chicken to the pan and simmer for 2 minutes. Season and serve with rice, if you like.

Ingredients

2 boneless, skinless chicken breasts, sliced into strips
1 tsp honey
1 tbsp olive oil

Sauce

1 tbsp apricot jam
1 tbsp mango chutney
4 tbsp crème fraîche
1 tsp Worcestershire sauce
1 tbsp lemon juice

Shopping list

Keep your fridge and cupboards stocked to save running to the shops mid-preparation. Have a shopping list pinned to the wall so that you can note down ingredients when they run out.

Ingredients

200 g (7 oz) tagliatelle
1 tbsp olive oil
225 g (8 oz) minced chicken
   or turkey
1 onion, chopped
1 garlic clove, crushed
2 tbsp plain flour
300 ml (½ pint) chicken stock
75 ml (3 fl oz) double cream
2 tsp soy sauce
2 tsp Worcestershire sauce
1 tsp chopped fresh thyme
2 tbsp snipped fresh chives

Tagliatelle Ragu

A classic pasta dish with a difference which my children love. Here I've used chicken or turkey mince for a less meaty flavour.

∗ Heat the oil in a saucepan, add the mince and onion and fry for 3–5 minutes. Add the garlic and fry for 30 seconds. Sprinkle over the flour, then blend in all the remaining ingredients except the chives. Cover and simmer for 15 minutes.

∗ Meanwhile, cook the pasta in a pan of boiling lightly salted water according to the packet instructions. Drain, then add to the sauce with the chives, tossing it to coat.

Quick Chicken Nuggets

Makes approx. 25 nuggets

Instead of dipping chicken nuggets in beaten egg and seasoned flour, I coat them in pesto, which gives them a delicious flavour.

★ Preheat the oven to 200°C/180°C Fan/400°F/Gas 6.

★ Slice the chicken breasts into small cubes – you should get 10–12 pieces from each breast. Put the chicken into a bowl, season, and mix in the pesto.

★ Put the cornflakes into a plastic food bag and bash them with a rolling pin to make fine crumbs. Add the cheese and half of the chicken to the bag. Shake the bag to coat the nuggets, then transfer them to a plate. Add the remaining chicken to the bag of crumbs and repeat.

★ Lay the nuggets on a baking sheet and cook in the oven for 10 minutes.

Ingredients

2 boneless, skinless
  chicken breasts
2 tbsp red pesto
50 g (2 oz) cornflakes
15 g (½ oz) Parmesan,
  finely grated

Quick Chicken and Gravy

Ingredients

2 boneless, skinless chicken
  breasts, sliced into strips
2 tsp Worcestershire sauce
1 tsp honey
1 tbsp olive oil

For the gravy
1 onion, sliced
½ tsp honey
300 ml (½ pint) chicken stock
1 tsp Worcestershire sauce
1 tsp soy sauce
1 tsp dried thyme
1 tsp cornflour

Coating the chicken in honey and Worcestershire sauce gives it a lovely flavour. Serve this with an onion gravy flavoured with soy sauce, honey and thyme and perhaps some shop-bought mashed potato. If you can get one, try a variation like potato mashed with carrot.

✴ Season the chicken and coat it in the Worcestershire sauce and honey. Heat the oil in a frying pan and cook the chicken until cooked through and golden. Remove from the pan using a slotted spoon and set aside.

✴ Meanwhile, make the gravy. Cook the onion in the pan in the hot oil and fry for 5–8 minutes until soft. Add the honey and cook for a few seconds. Add the stock, Worcestershire sauce, soy sauce and thyme and bring to the boil. Mix the cornflour with a few tablespoons of cold water in a small bowl, pour this into the sauce and stir over the heat until thickened. Return the chicken to the pan and simmer all together for 2 minutes.

Chicken Balls with Pasta and Broccoli

Makes 5 portions

A tasty meal for the whole family. Take care not to overcook the broccoli, it only needs 4 minutes' cooking.

✴ To make the chicken balls, put the bread into a bowl, pour over the milk, leave to soak for 5 minutes, then mash with a fork. Add the mince, chives, Parmesan and seasoning, mix together, then shape into 20 small balls using your hands. Spread the flour over a plate and gently roll the meatballs in it until evenly coated. Heat a little oil in a frying pan and fry for 8–10 minutes until cooked and golden brown.

✴ Cook the pasta in a pan of boiling lightly salted water according to the packet instructions. About 4 minutes before the end of the cooking time, add the broccoli. Drain.

✴ For the sauce, heat the oil in a frying pan and fry the onion for 5 minutes. Add the garlic and cook for 30 seconds, then add the stock, bring the liquid up to the boil and allow it to reduce a little. Add the cream and bubble for 3 minutes. In a small bowl, mix the cornflour with 2 tablespoons of water and add to the pan, stirring to thicken. Tip in the pasta, broccoli, meatballs, Parmesan, chives and lemon juice and simmer for 2 minutes. Season to taste, then serve.

Ingredients

200 g (7 oz) fusilli
100 g (3½ oz) broccoli florets

Chicken balls

50 g (2 oz) white bread
4 tbsp milk
300 g (11 oz) minced chicken
   or turkey
2 tbsp snipped fresh chives
30 g (1 oz) Parmesan, grated
plain flour, for dusting

Sauce

1 tbsp oil
1 onion, chopped
1 garlic clove, crushed
300 ml (½ pint) chicken stock
100 ml (3½ fl oz) double cream
2 tsp cornflour
30 g (1 oz) Parmesan, grated
2 tbsp snipped fresh chives
juice of ½ small lemon

Meat

Sticky Lamb Chops

Chops are a quick-cook cut of meat and children love them as they stay tender and juicy. This is a simple way to serve them with maximum flavour.

Ingredients

Makes 4 portions

4 small lamb chops
3 tbsp redcurrant jelly
1½ tsp Dijon mustard

✳ Preheat the oven to 220°C/200°C Fan/425°F/Gas 7.

✳ Put the lamb chops onto a baking sheet lined with non-stick paper. Mix the redcurrant jelly and Dijon mustard together until smooth. Spoon the mixture over the chops and spread it out so that they are completely covered.

✳ Roast the chops in the oven for 15–18 minutes or until golden and sticky, basting halfway through.

Sausage and Bean Hot Pot

A hearty feast on a chilly day. This really quick version of the popular one-pot is simply sausages with my home-made version of baked beans. Your children will love it.

Ingredients

Makes 3 portions

2 tsp oil
1 onion, finely chopped
1 garlic clove, crushed
500 g (1 lb 2 oz) passata
½ tsp Worcestershire sauce
½ tsp brown sugar
3 tbsp ketchup
1 tsp thyme
1 x 400 g can haricot beans, drained
6 good-quality cooked sausages

✳ Heat the oil in a saucepan. Add the onion and cook for 5 minutes, then add the garlic and fry for 30 seconds. Add the remaining ingredients, except the sausages and bring to the boil, then simmer for 5 minutes.

✳ Slice each sausage into three, add them to the saucepan and simmer everything together for 5 minutes.

✳ Serve with ready-made mash.

Meatballs in Goulash Sauce

Ingredients

50 g (2 oz) white bread, torn into pieces
4 tbsp milk
225 g (8 oz) minced beef
1 tsp chopped fresh thyme
30 (1 oz) Parmesan, grated

Sauce

1 tbsp sunflower oil
1 onion, finely chopped
1 red pepper, deseeded and diced
½ tsp sweet smoked paprika
1 garlic clove, crushed
150 ml (5 fl oz) beef stock
1 x 400 g can chopped tomatoes
2 tsp Worcestershire sauce
2 tsp sundried tomato paste
2 tbsp crème fraîche

There's no need to spend extra time frying the meatballs in this recipe; simply drop them into the sauce to cook.

✳ To make the meatballs, put the bread into a bowl, pour over the milk and leave to soak for 5 minutes. Mash the bread with a fork, then add the mince, thyme and cheese. Season and shape the mixture into 20 small balls using your hands.

✳ To make the sauce, heat the oil in a saucepan and fry the onion and pepper for 5 minutes. Add the paprika and garlic and fry for 1 minute, then add all the remaining ingredients and bring to the boil. Add the meatballs, cover the pan with a lid and simmer for 15 minutes until the meatballs are cooked through. Serve with rice.

Plan ahead

Whenever possible make double the quantity and freeze extra portions.

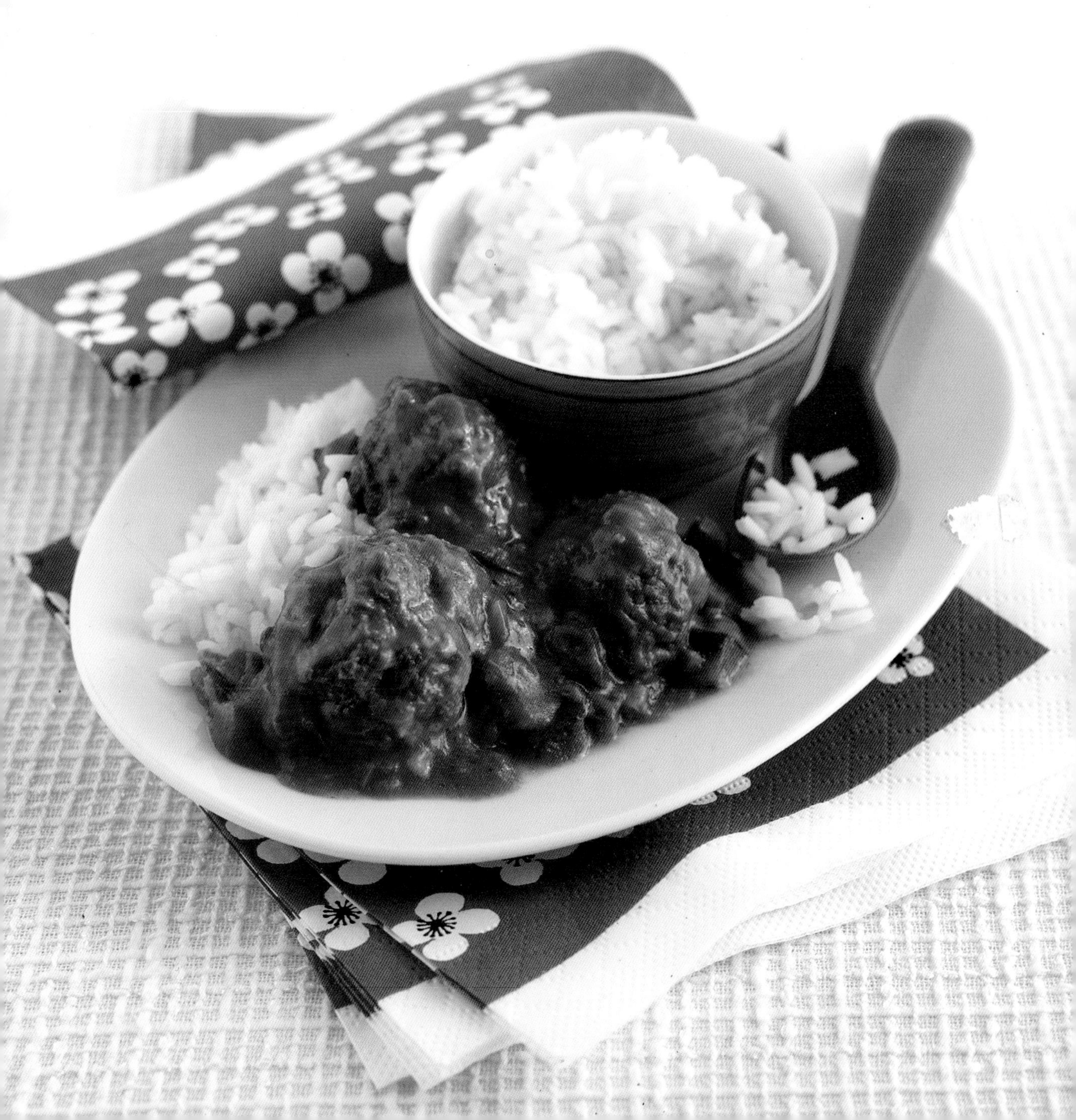

Ham, Mozzarella and Pesto Tortilla Sandwiches

This is a warming sandwich on a cold day and a delicious twist on a ham and cheese toastie.

Ingredients

2 tortilla wraps
1 tbsp pesto
1 slice ham
½ tomato, thinly sliced
½ x 125 g ball mozzarella, sliced

Makes 2 portions

★ Spread 1 wrap with pesto and top with the ham, tomato slices and mozzarella. Put the other wrap on top and press down to make a sandwich.

★ Heat a frying pan until hot and fry the sandwich for a few minutes on both sides until lightly golden and the cheese has melted. Slice into 6 wedges.

Ham, Potato and Tomato Croquettes

Ingredients

200 g (7 oz) ready-made mashed potato
6 spring onions, finely chopped
2 tbsp chopped fresh basil
50 g (2 oz) ham, finely chopped
30 g (1 oz) Parmesan, grated
100 g (3½ oz) fresh white breadcrumbs
30 g (1 oz) sunblush tomatoes, chopped
a little oil, for frying

Makes 8 croquettes

★ Put the potato, spring onions, basil, ham and Parmesan in a bowl, and add half of the breadcrumbs and all the sunblush tomatoes. Mix everything together and season. Shape the mixture into 8 small sausage shapes then roll each one in the remaining breadcrumbs.

★ Heat a little oil in a frying pan and fry the croquettes for about 5 minutes or until golden brown and crispy.

Ready-made mash
Buy ready-made mashed potato from the supermarket.

Pork Fillet Stir-Fry

Makes 4 portions

This meal in minutes is made super-quick by using ready-cooked noodles and pre-prepared stir-fry veg, but you can add other veg if you prefer.

✶ Heat half the oil in a frying pan or wok. Season the pork, then quickly fry until brown and just cooked. Remove from the pan and set aside.

✶ Heat the remaining oil in the pan, and stir-fry the garlic, then tip in the noodles and vegetables. Fry for 3 minutes.

✶ Meanwhile, mix the sauce ingredients together. Add the sauce and pork to the wok and stir-fry everything together for 2 minutes. Serve at once.

Ingredients

2 tbsp oil
200 g (7 oz) pork fillet, sliced into strips
1 garlic clove, crushed
150 g (5 oz) fresh cooked noodles from a packet
1 x 350 g packet stir-fry vegetables

Sauce

1 tbsp oyster sauce
1 tbsp soy sauce
2 tsp honey
1 tbsp hoisin sauce

Making stir-fries

Have all the ingredients prepared ahead of time, as once cooking there is no time to measure or chop. Start with the veg that takes the longest to cook, like onions and carrots, and make sure you stir-fry continuously so that the vegetables cook evenly and don't burn. To save time buy ready-prepared stir-fry vegetables.

Quick BBQ Steak

Ingredients

2 tsp sunflower oil
1 onion, finely chopped
1 garlic clove, crushed
3 tbsp ketchup
1 tbsp soy sauce
2 tsp brown sugar
1 tsp Worcestershire sauce
½ tsp balsamic vinegar
150 ml (5 fl oz) water
1 tsp cornflour
250 g (9 oz) sirloin steak

Bashing out the steaks to make thin strips means the meat will cook in minutes.

✳ To make the sauce, heat half the oil and sauté the onion for 5 minutes until soft. Add the garlic and fry for 1 minute. Add the ketchup, soy sauce, sugar, Worcestershire sauce, vinegar and 100 ml of the water.

✳ Mix the remaining 50 ml of water with the cornflour in a small bowl and add this to the sauce, then bring it to the boil and simmer for 2 minutes.

✳ Lay the steak out on a chopping board and cover it with cling film. Bash the meat out very thinly using a rolling pin, then slice it into strips. Heat the remaining oil in a frying pan and fry the strips quickly over a high heat until just cooked. Add these to the sauce and remove from the heat.

✳ Serve with vegetables and rice.

Annabel's Burgers

Ingredients

1 tbsp sunflower oil
1 onion, peeled and finely chopped
450 g (1 lb) lean minced beef
1 tbsp chopped fresh parsley or 2 tsp fresh thyme
1 chicken stock cube, finely crumbled
1 apple, peeled and grated
1 egg, lightly beaten
50 g (2 oz) fresh breadcrumbs
1 tsp Worcestershire sauce
flour, for dusting
butter, or Marmite,
    for grilling (optional)

Makes 8 burgers Suitable for freezing

✳ Heat the oil in a frying pan and sauté the onion for about 5 minutes or until softened. In a mixing bowl, combine all the remaining ingredients except the flour, butter and Marmite. Add the onion once it has cooled a little. Season.

✳ Preheat the grill to high. With floured hands, form the mixture into 8 burgers and arrange them on a baking sheet lined with foil. Top each one with a knob of butter and a little Marmite if liked. Cook the burgers under the grill – they should be quite close to the heat – for about 5 minutes on each side or until cooked through.

✳ Serve the burgers on their own or in a toasted hamburger bun with salad and ketchup.

Onion Rings

These are good served with Annabel's Burgers (see left).

Makes 4 portions

Ingredients

About 750 ml (1¼ pints) sunflower oil, for frying
2 medium onions, sliced into rings

Batter

100 g (3½ oz) plain flour
1 egg
1 egg yolk
150 ml (5 fl oz) milk
¼ tsp salt

✳ Mix the flour, egg, egg yolk, milk and salt together to make a smooth batter.

✳ Heat the oil in a deep frying pan. Dip the onion rings in the batter, shaking off the excess, and fry in the hot oil until golden. You may need to do this in batches. Remove with a slotted spoon to a plate lined with kitchen paper and serve immediately.

Making breadcrumbs

When making fresh breadcrumbs make more than you need and freeze any extra in a sealed freezer bag. You can also freeze crumble topping in the same way.

Veal Schnitzel

Makes 2 portions

Adding Parmesan and fresh thyme to the breadcrumbs gives them a lovely flavour. These are good served with spaghetti and tomato sauce.

✳ Put the veal onto a chopping board and cover the cutlets with cling film. Bash out the meat using a rolling pin so that the pieces are very thin.

✳ Whiz the bread in a food processor to make the breadcrumbs, then tip them into a bowl and add the Parmesan and thyme. Put the beaten egg on one plate and the breadcrumb mixture on another, then dip the veal first into beaten egg, then into the breadcrumbs, coating them so the meat is completely covered.

✳ Heat the oil in a frying pan. Fry the schnitzels for 5 minutes, turning them over halfway through. You may need to do this in batches. Serve immediately.

Ingredients

2 x 125 g (4 oz) veal cutlets
1 slice white bread
1 tbsp grated Parmesan
¼ tsp chopped fresh thyme
1 egg, beaten
1 tbsp olive oil

Beef, Broccoli and Corn Stir-Fry

Ingredients

75 g (3 oz) noodles
2 tbsp sunflower oil
200 g (7 oz) sirloin steak,
   thinly sliced
75 g (3 oz) baby corn,
   cut into quarters
75 g (3 oz) broccoli florets
1 tsp grated fresh root ginger
2 tbsp soy sauce
1 tbsp honey

The honey and soy sauce in this recipe give this a sweet and sour flavour. If time is really tight, serve with straight-to-wok noodles.

✳ Cook the noodles in a pan of boiling water according to the packet instructions. Drain.

✳ Heat half the oil in a wok. Season the beef and fry for a few minutes until cooked and golden. Transfer to a plate.

✳ Add the remaining oil to a frying pan and fry the corn and broccoli for 3 minutes. Add the ginger and fry for 1 minute. Add the noodles and beef and season to taste. Pour in the soy sauce and honey and toss everything together. Serve immediately.

Teriyaki Beef Stir-Fry

Ingredients

300 g (11 oz) sirloin steak
2 tbsp sesame oil
6 spring onions, sliced
100 g (3½ oz) baby corn, sliced
1 red pepper, deseeded
   and sliced
75 g (3 oz) sugar snap
   peas, sliced
½ tsp finely grated fresh root
   ginger

Sauce

4 tbsp soy sauce
2 tbsp honey
2 tbsp rice wine vinegar
2 tsp cornflour

You can cheat by using a ready-prepared selection of stir-fry vegetables, or pick the ones you know your child likes. You can serve this with straight-to-wok noodles if you like (see photograph, opposite). Just add them to the pan for the last minute of cooking time

★ Place the steak on a chopping board and cover with cling film. Bash the meat until thin using a rolling pin. Season and cut into strips.

★ Heat 1 tablespoon of oil in a frying pan and quickly fry the beef until just cooked and browned. Transfer to a plate. Heat the remaining oil in the pan, add all the vegetables and stir-fry for 4 minutes, then add the ginger.

★ Mix all of the sauce ingredients together, then pour the mixture over the vegetables, return the beef to the pan and toss everything together over the heat for 1 minute. Serve at once.

Sweet and Sour Pork

Makes 4 portions
Suitable for freezing

This is a quick version of sweet and sour, and really simple to make. Serve this on a bed of express rice.

✳ Heat half the oil in a frying pan. Season the pork, then quickly fry until sealed and just cooked. Transfer to a plate. Heat the remaining oil in the pan, and fry the onion for 3 minutes, then add the pepper and carrots and fry for 5 minutes. Finally, add the garlic and cook for 1 minute.

✳ Mix all of the sauce ingredients together until blended, then pour this over the vegetables. Bring to the boil, return the pork to the pan along with the pineapple chunks and simmer everything together for 3 minutes.

Ingredients

2 tbsp olive oil
300 g (11 oz) pork fillet, sliced into strips
1 onion, chopped
½ red pepper, diced
2 small carrots, sliced
1 garlic clove, crushed
75 g (3 oz) pineapple chunks

Sauce

5 tbsp ketchup
2 tbsp soy sauce
2 tbsp rice wine vinegar
1½ tsp brown sugar
250 ml (8 fl oz) water
1 tbsp cornflour

Vegetables

Butternut Squash and Sweetcorn Soup

Let's face it, butternut squash is quite hard to peel, however you can buy peeled and chopped butternut squash in the supermarket, which makes life much easier.

Ingredients

1 tbsp olive oil
1 large onion, chopped
2 garlic cloves, crushed
500 g (1 lb 2 oz) peeled
   butternut squash, cubed
175 g (6 oz) canned sweetcorn, drained
600 ml (1 pint) chicken or vegetable stock
1 tsp chopped fresh thyme
3 tbsp crème fraîche

Makes 6 portions Suitable for freezing

✳ Heat the oil in a saucepan and fry the onion for 3 minutes. Add the garlic, butternut squash and sweetcorn and fry for 2 minutes. Add the stock and thyme and bring to the boil. Cover with a lid and simmer for 15 minutes until the squash is tender.

✳ Blend the soup until smooth, then add the crème fraîche and season.

Vegetarian Toasted Tortilla Sandwich

Ingredients

1 tbsp olive oil
1 large red onion, thinly sliced
1 small red pepper, deseeded
   and thinly sliced
1 tsp balsamic vinegar
1 tsp brown sugar
4 tortilla wraps
2 tbsp sundried tomato paste
50 g (2 oz) mature Cheddar, grated

Makes 4 portions

✳ Heat the oil in a frying pan and fry the onion gently for 5 minutes. Add the pepper and cook for another 5 minutes until soft. Add the vinegar and sugar and stir over the heat. Season.

✳ Spread two wraps with the tomato paste, put the onion mixture on top and sprinkle with cheese. Put the other wraps on top and press down. Heat a frying pan, and fry the sandwiches for a few minutes on both sides until lightly golden and the cheese has melted. Slice each sandwich into 6 wedges to serve.

Ingredients

1 tbsp olive oil
1 large stick celery,
  finely chopped
1 leek, chopped
½ red pepper, deseeded
  and diced
2 carrots, diced finely
175 g (6 oz) peeled butternut
  squash, diced
1 tbsp curry paste
1 tbsp tomato purée
1 litre (1¾ pints) chicken stock
1 tsp caster sugar
2 small bay leaves
50 g (2 oz) long grain rice

Mulligatawny Soup

Adding a hint of curry gives this tasty soup a little kick.

✳ Heat the oil in a deep saucepan and fry all the vegetables together for 5 minutes. Add the curry paste and tomato purée and fry for 1 minute.

✳ Add the stock, sugar and bay leaves. Bring to the boil, then simmer for 15–20 minutes until all the vegetables are cooked. Season. Remove the bay leaves and blend the soup until smooth using an electric hand blender.

✳ Cook the rice in a pan of boiling water according to the packet instructions, drain, then add to the soup.

Save time on veg
Buy ready-prepared
chopped vegetables.

Tagliatelle with Cherry Tomatoes, Spinach and Peas

Ingredients

200 g (7 oz) tagliatelle
50 g (2 oz) frozen peas
a knob of butter, for frying
1 large onion, thinly sliced
2 garlic cloves, crushed
200 ml (7 fl oz) chicken
   or vegetable stock
100 g (3½ oz) crème fraîche
75 g (3 oz) baby leaf spinach
150 g (5 oz) cherry tomatoes,
   halved
50 g (2 oz) Parmesan, grated,
   plus extra for serving
   (optional)

A very quick and easy pasta sauce which is colourful and healthy too.

✳ Cook the pasta in a pan of boiling lightly salted water according to the packet instructions. About 4 minutes before the end of the cooking time, add the peas. Drain.

✳ While the pasta is cooking, make the sauce. Heat the butter in a frying pan and gently fry the onion for 5 minutes until soft. Add the garlic and fry for 2 minutes. Add the stock and crème fraîche, bring to the boil and then cook over a high heat for 2 minutes to reduce. Add the spinach, pasta and peas and toss over the heat. Season and add the tomatoes and Parmesan.

✳ Heat everything through in the pan, then serve at once with extra Parmesan cheese scattered over, if liked.

Tomato and Basil Risotto

Makes 4 portions

You can buy quick-cook long grain rice, which cooks perfectly in just 10 minutes.

Ingredients

100 g (3½ oz) long grain rice
1 tbsp olive oil
1 onion, finely chopped
1 garlic clove, crushed
150 ml (5 fl oz) vegetable or chicken stock
6 sunblush tomatoes, chopped
1 large tomato, deseeded and diced
2 tsp sundried tomato paste
2 tbsp chopped fresh basil
30 g (1 oz) Parmesan, grated

✳ Cook the rice in a pan of boiling water according to the packet instructions.

✳ While the rice is cooking, heat the oil in a saucepan and fry the onion for 5 minutes until soft. Add the garlic and fry for 30 seconds. Add the stock, then drain the rice and add to the pan. Add the remaining ingredients and stir over the heat for 1–2 minutes. Season to taste.

Stir-Fried Vegetables

Makes 4 portions

Ingredients

1 tbsp sunflower oil
50 g (2 oz) broccoli, broken into florets
100 g (3½ oz) carrots, sliced into thin strips
½ yellow pepper, deseeded and sliced
1 courgette, sliced into thin strips
4 spring onions, sliced

Sauce

1 tbsp soy sauce
2 tbsp tomato ketchup
2 tbsp rice wine vinegar
2 tbsp caster sugar
½ tsp sesame oil

✳ Heat the oil in a large frying pan, add all of the vegetables and stir-fry for 5 minutes.

✳ Meanwhile, mix all of the sauce ingredients together, then pour this over the vegetables and season. Toss everything together and serve at once.

Use a food processor
Chop vegetables in a food processor to save time.

Courgette and Carrot Risotto

It's quick and easy to make a delicious risotto when you use express rice.

✶ Heat the oil in a frying pan and fry the onion, carrot and courgette for about 8 minutes until soft. Add the garlic and fry for 30 seconds.

✶ Cook the rice in a microwave according to the packet instructions. Add the rice to the pan with the stock and stir for 1 minute, then add the chives and Parmesan. Season to taste.

Ingredients

1 tbsp olive oil
1 onion, chopped
1 carrot, grated
1 courgette, finely diced
1 garlic clove, crushed
1 x 250 g packet express basmati rice
200 ml (7 fl oz) chicken stock
1 tbsp snipped fresh chives
30 g (1 oz) Parmesan, grated

Fresh herbs

When using fresh herbs like chives, dill or parsley, hold them together in small bunches and snip with kitchen scissors. It's much quicker than chopping and the herbs will not be bruised or wet.

Macaroni Cheese with Broccoli and Sunblush Tomatoes

Ingredients

150 g (5 oz) macaroni
150 g (5 oz) cauliflower florets
100 g (3½ oz) broccoli florets
40 g (1½ oz) butter
40 g (1½ oz) plain flour
450 ml (16 fl oz) milk
100 g (3½ oz) mature Cheddar,
　grated
10 sunblush tomatoes,
　roughly chopped

Here's a clever way to sneak some veggies into one of your child's favourite dishes...

✶ Cook the macaroni in a pan of boiling lightly salted water according to the packet instructions. About 4 minutes before the end of the cooking time, add the cauliflower and broccoli. Drain.

✶ While the pasta is cooking, make the cheese sauce. Melt the butter in a saucepan and add the flour, stirring. Whisk in the milk until smooth and thickened. Season and add the cheese.

✶ Tip the pasta into the sauce with the tomatoes. Serve at once or, if you wish, you can pop the dish under a hot grill for 3–4 minutes to brown the top.

Frittata

Make this for dinner and pop a wedge into your child's lunchbox the next day.

Ingredients

Makes 6 portions

2 tbsp sunflower oil
1 large onion, sliced
1 red pepper, deseeded and diced
150 g (5 oz) cooked potatoes, diced
1 garlic clove, crushed
1 large tomato, deseeded and sliced
5 large eggs
2 tbsp chopped fresh basil
30 g (1 oz) Parmesan, grated

✱ Preheat the oven to 200°C/180°C Fan/ 400°F/Gas 6.

✱ Heat the oil in a large frying pan with an ovenproof handle, add the onion and pepper and cook, stirring, for 5–8 minutes until soft and lightly golden. Add the potatoes, garlic and tomato and fry for 1 minute.

✱ Mix the eggs, basil and Parmesan together, season, and pour this mixture over the vegetables. Gently fry for 2 minutes until the egg is set around the sides. Transfer the pan to the oven for 10 minutes until just set. Flip out onto a plate and slice into wedges.

Roasted Vegetable Pasta with Mozzarella

Roasting vegetables caramelises their natural sweetness. Combine the veg with creamy mini mozzarella balls and a tasty dressing to create a delicious pasta dish.

Ingredients

**Makes 4 portions
Suitable for freezing**

200 g (7 oz) penne
2 small courgettes, chopped
½ red and ½ yellow pepper, deseeded and diced
½ red onion, sliced thinly
2 tbsp olive oil
2 tomatoes, deseeded and chopped
250 g (9 oz) mozzarella, cubed, or use mini mozzarella balls
2 handfuls of fresh basil leaves, chopped
3 tbsp sundried tomato paste
2 tsp rice wine vinegar

✱ Preheat the oven to 220°C/200°C Fan/ 425°F/ Gas 7. Put the courgettes, peppers and onion on a baking tray, drizzle with the olive oil and season. Roast for 20 minutes until tinged brown.

✱ Cook the pasta in a pan of boiling lightly salted water according to the packet instructions. Drain, reserving 3 tablespoons of water. Add the vegetables to the pasta with the remaining ingredients and the reserved pasta cooking water. Toss together and season.

Spinach and Ricotta Pancakes

Makes 4 portions
Suitable for freezing

Present these and it looks like you've spent ages in the kitchen, but actually they are really quick to prepare, especially when you use delicious ready-made pancakes.

✷ Preheat the oven to 220°C/200°C Fan/425°F/Gas 7.

✷ Cook the spinach in a hot frying pan until wilted. Drain in a colander, pushing out any liquid, then mix the wilted leaves with the ricotta, Parmesan and some seasoning.

✷ Divide the mixture into 4, then put the pancakes on a chopping board and spoon the mixture along the middle of each. Roll up each pancake and place them side by side in a shallow ovenproof dish.

✷ Mix the tomatoes, tomato paste and basil together, pour the sauce over the pancakes and sprinkle with the Cheddar. Bake for 15–20 minutes until bubbling.

Ingredients

250 g (9 oz) baby spinach
1 x 250 g tub ricotta cheese
50 g (2 oz) Parmesan, grated
4 ready-made pancakes
1 x 400 g can chopped
   tomatoes
1 tbsp sundried tomato paste
2 tbsp chopped fresh basil
50 g (2 oz) Cheddar, grated

Couscous Salad

Ingredients

200 g (7 oz) couscous
450 ml (16 fl oz) hot chicken
   or vegetable stock
75 g (3 oz) cooked French
   beans, chopped
75 g (3 oz) carrot, grated
6 spring onions, sliced
2 tomatoes, deseeded
   and diced
75 g (3 oz) canned sweetcorn,
   drained

Dressing

1 tbsp rice wine vinegar
1 tsp honey
1½ tbsp olive oil

You can combine couscous with many ingredients to make delicious salads, so pick your favourites, if you prefer! You could substitute some diced red pepper for the tomatoes, and dried cranberries are also good in salads.

✳ Put the couscous into a bowl and pour over the hot stock. Cover the bowl with cling film and leave to stand for 10 minutes or until all of the stock has been absorbed.

✳ Add the vegetables to the couscous and season. Combine the ingredients for the salad dressing and pour this over the salad, mixing everything together well.

Carrot, Courgette and Sweetcorn Fritters

Makes 8-10 fritters

A tasty way to encourage children to eat their veggies.

✳ Beat the egg in a mixing bowl then beat in the flour and milk until smooth. Add the remaining ingredients and season.

✳ Heat the oil in a frying pan. Take spoonfuls of the mixture and fry them for 2–3 minutes each side until lightly golden, turning over halfway through. You may have to do this in batches, so keep the cooked fritters warm while you cook the rest.

Ingredients

1 egg
50 g (2 oz) self-raising flour
1 tbsp milk
1 tbsp sweet chilli sauce
100 g (3½ oz) courgette, grated
50 g (2 oz) carrot, grated
4 spring onions, sliced
2 tbsp canned sweetcorn, drained
50 g (2 oz) mature Cheddar, grated
a little oil, for frying

English Muffin Pizzas

Ingredients

1 tbsp olive oil

½ red onion, chopped

½ small red pepper, deseeded and diced

½ small yellow pepper, deseeded and diced

50 g (2 oz) courgette, diced

50 g (2 oz) brown mushrooms, diced

1 tsp chopped fresh thyme

1 tsp garlic purée

2 English muffins

4 tbsp passata

1 tbsp sundried tomato paste

30 g (1 oz) Cheddar, grated

30 g (1 oz) mozzarella, grated

black olives, fresh basil leaves, mini mozzarella balls, pieces of red pepper, to decorate (optional)

Split toasted English muffins make good individual pizza bases when you're in a hurry. And by topping them yourself you can sneak in some extra veggies...

✳ Preheat the grill.

✳ Heat the oil in a frying pan and fry the onion, peppers, courgette and mushrooms for 8 minutes until soft and lightly golden brown. Add the thyme and garlic and fry for 1 minute.

✳ Slice the muffins in half and arrange the halves on a baking sheet, cut side up. Mix the passata and sundried tomato paste together and spread over the muffins. Spoon over the mixed vegetables, then sprinkle the tops with the cheeses.

✳ Grill for 4–5 minutes until the cheese has melted and is bubbling. Decorate with food 'faces' before serving, if liked.

Fruit

Three-Melon Fruit Salad

Makes 4 portions

This salad looks lovely if you make it using three different-coloured melons.

Ingredients

½ small watermelon
½ small Galia melon
½ small Cantaloupe melon

Syrup

50 g (2 oz) caster sugar
150 ml (5 fl oz) water
squeeze of lime juice

✳ Slice each melon in half and then into four quarters. Remove the rind and cut the quarters into slices.

✳ Next, make the syrup. Measure the sugar and water into a saucepan and stir together over the heat until dissolved. Leave to cool, then add the lime juice.

✳ Pour the cooled sauce over the slices of melon and chill until ready to serve.

Caramelised Banana and Mango

Fresh, ripe mangoes and bananas are delicious on their own, but for something special why not caramelise the fruit and serve warm with vanilla ice cream.

Ingredients

Makes 4 portions

50 g (2 oz) butter
50 g (2 oz) brown sugar
2 bananas, thickly sliced
1 mango, sliced into strips

✳ Melt the butter in a frying pan, add the sugar and stir until melted. Add the bananas and toss them over the heat for 1 minute. Add the mango and toss together for another minute. Remove from the heat and serve with vanilla ice cream.

Red Fruit Salad

Ingredients

a knob of butter, for frying
3 tbsp brown sugar
180 g (6 oz) blueberries
150 g (5 oz) raspberries
200 g (7 oz) strawberries

Makes 4 portions

✶ Melt the butter in a saucepan, add the sugar and stir over the heat. Add the blueberries and cook, stirring, for 3 minutes until they start to soften. Remove from the heat and add the raspberries and strawberries. Mix everything together gently and leave to cool.

Fruit Compote

Ingredients

a knob of butter, for frying
175 g (6 oz) peaches, sliced
100 g (3½ oz) blueberries
75 g (3 oz) caster sugar
100 g (3½ oz) strawberries, quartered
100 g (3½ oz) raspberries
a spoonful of ice cream or
  Greek yoghurt, to serve

Makes 4 portions

✶ Melt the butter in a saucepan, then add the peaches and stir them gently over the heat for 30 seconds. Add the blueberries and sugar and stir for 1 minute. Remove from the heat and add the strawberries and raspberries.

✶ Serve with ice cream or Greek yoghurt. (See photograph opposite.)

Ripening fruit
Fruit bought in supermarkets is often unripe and hard. To help ripen put the fruit in a brown paper bag and store in a dark place for a day or two.

Quick Flapjacks

Ingredients

75 g (3 oz) butter
75 g (3 oz) soft brown sugar
50 g (2 oz) golden syrup
225 g (8 oz) Swiss-style muesli
   with fruit
30 g (1 oz) desiccated coconut

A tasty flapjack that takes minutes to prepare.

✳ Preheat the oven to 180°C/160°C Fan/350°F/Gas 4.
Lightly butter an 18-cm (7-inch) square non-stick baking tin.

✳ Melt the butter, sugar and syrup together in a saucepan.
Remove from the heat and add the muesli and coconut.
Mix everything together and spoon into the prepared
baking tin. Level the top, then bake in the oven for
12 minutes.

✳ Leave to cool in the tin for 15 minutes before cutting
into 16 squares. Turn out onto a wire rack and leave to
cool completely.

Measuring golden syrup

When measuring golden syrup heat
the spoon in hot water beforehand
to make it slide off easily.

Blueberry, Pear and Apple Crumble

Ingredients

a knob of butter (about 30 g/1 oz)
2 large ripe pears, peeled and diced
3 dessert apples (e.g. Braeburn or Pink Lady),
    peeled and diced
175 g (6 oz) blueberries
3 tbsp light brown sugar
¼ tsp ground cinnamon

Crumble topping

100 g (3½ oz) plain flour
75 g (3 oz) butter, cubed
50 g (2 oz) ground almonds
50 g (2 oz) light brown sugar

Makes 4 portions

★ Preheat the oven to 200°C/180°C Fan/
400°F/Gas 6.

★ Melt the butter in a frying pan, then add the fruit and sugar and fry over a high heat for 4–5 minutes. Spoon into a shallow ovenproof dish and sprinkle with the cinnamon.

★ To make the topping, combine the flour, butter, ground almonds and sugar in a mixing bowl. Rub in the butter using your fingers until the mixture looks like breadcrumbs.

★ Spread the crumble over the fruits and bake in the oven for 20 minutes until bubbling and lightly golden on top.

Rhubarb Crumble

I've always liked the slightly tart taste of rhubarb with a sweet crumble topping.

Ingredients

50 g (2 oz) butter
500 g (1lb 2 oz) rhubarb, chopped
    into 2-cm (¾-in) pieces
75 g (3 oz) caster sugar
6 tbsp fresh orange juice or water

Crumble topping

75 g (3 oz) salted butter
150 g (5 oz) plain flour
60 g (2½ oz) demerara sugar

Makes 4 individual crumbles

★ Preheat the oven to 180°C/160°C Fan/
350°F/Gas 4.

★ Melt the butter in a saucepan and cook the rhubarb, sugar and orange juice or water for about 10 minutes until the rhubarb is soft but still holding its shape. Spoon the fruit into 4 individual ramekins.

★ Rub the butter into the flour until the mixture looks like breadcrumbs, then stir in the demerara sugar. Spoon the crumble mix on top of the fruit and bake in the oven for 15 minutes until bubbling.

Peach and Raspberry Crumble

Ingredients

a knob of butter, for frying
2 large ripe peaches,
  chopped into cubes
50 g (2 oz) light brown sugar
150 g (5 oz) raspberries

Crumble topping

150 g (5 oz) plain flour
75 g (3 oz) butter, cubed
50 g (2 oz) brown sugar

When sweet, ripe peaches are in season this is one of my favourite crumbles.

✳ Preheat the oven to 180°C/160°C Fan/350°F/Gas 4.

✳ Melt the butter in a saucepan and add the peaches, then sprinkle over the sugar. Cook, stirring gently, over the heat for 2 minutes. Add the raspberries, then tip the fruit into 4 individual ramekins.

✳ Put the flour and butter into a bowl and rub together until it looks like breadcrumbs. Stir in the sugar, then sprinkle the crumble on top of the fruit. Bake in the oven for 15 minutes until lightly golden and bubbling around the edges.

Apple and Sultana Muffins

Ingredients

125 g (4 oz) butter, softened
125 g (4 oz) caster sugar
1 egg
200 ml (7 fl oz) milk
¼ tsp salt
225 g (8 oz) plain flour
1 tbsp baking powder
½ tsp ground ginger
1 tsp ground cinnamon
150 g (5 oz) dessert apples,
    peeled and grated
75 g (3 oz) sultanas
a little demerara sugar

These are fun to make together with your little one. The grated apple keeps the muffins lovely and moist. To freeze, interleave them with greaseproof baking paper and store in a plastic freezer box.

✳ Preheat the oven to 200°C/180°C Fan/400°F/Gas 6 and line a 12-hole muffin tin with paper cases.

✳ Measure all of the ingredients, except the demerara sugar, into a free-standing mixer and whisk until combined. Spoon the batter into the paper cases until almost full and sprinkle over the demerara sugar. Bake in the oven for 20–22 minutes until well risen and lightly golden.

✳ Remove from the oven and allow to cool for 5 minutes, then transfer to a wire rack to cool completely.

Chocolate Raspberry Mousse

Makes 4 glasses

★ Melt the chocolate in a bowl set over a pan of just-simmering water. Stir until melted and smooth, then remove from the pan and leave to cool.

★ Whisk the cream until it forms soft peaks, then fold it into the cooled melted chocolate.

★ To make the coulis, put the raspberries and icing sugar into a blender and whiz until smooth. Sieve the mixture into a bowl.

★ To assemble the mousses, put four raspberries into each of the four glasses. Spoon half the mousse mixture on top, then drizzle over half the coulis. Put four raspberries on top of the coulis and spoon in the remaining mousse. Drizzle over the rest of the coulis to finish and top each with one raspberry.

Ingredients

150 g (5 oz) milk chocolate
200 ml (7 fl oz) whipping cream
150 g (5 oz) raspberries

Raspberry coulis

100 g (3½ oz) raspberries
30 g (1 oz) icing sugar

Ingredients

150 ml (5 fl oz) whipping
    cream
200 g (7 oz) Greek yoghurt
75 g (3 oz) bought meringues,
    broken into pieces
1 large ripe peach, diced
200 g (7 oz) raspberries

Eton Mess

This is a variation on the traditional Eton Mess – an
English dessert consisting of a mixture of strawberries,
meringue and cream which is served at Eton College
on 4 June to mark the start of summer.

✳ Whip the cream until it forms soft peaks, then add the
yoghurt and mix until smooth. Fold in all the remaining
ingredients (reserving a few raspberries and pieces of
peach and meringue for garnish) until evenly combined,
then spoon it into 4 individual serving glasses. Chill for
15 minutes before garnishing and serving.

Sultana Drop Scones

These make a great teatime treat. If you like, you can add a little butter to the oil when frying the drop scones, as it adds to the flavour.

★ Measure the flour, baking powder and caster sugar into a bowl, add the egg and milk and whisk together until smooth. Add the sultanas and mix them into the dough until evenly dispersed.

★ Heat a little oil in a frying pan, then spoon heaped tablespoons of the scone mixture into the pan and fry for a few minutes on each side until puffed up and lightly golden. Serve warm with butter or leave to cool and serve spread with jam.

Makes about 15
Suitable for freezing

Ingredients

225 g (8 oz) self-raising flour
1 tsp baking powder
50 g (2 oz) caster sugar
1 egg
200 ml (7 fl oz) milk
100 g (3½ oz) sultanas
a little sunflower oil, for frying

Steadying a mixing bowl

To keep a mixing bowl from sliding around while you are stirring or whisking, place on a damp kitchen towel.

Grilled Peach and Raspberry Pancakes

Ingredients

2 ready-made sweet pancakes
100 g (3½ oz) Greek yoghurt
1 ripe peach, diced
100 g (3½ oz) raspberries
1 tbsp caster sugar
2 tbsp apricot jam
20 g (¾ oz) Amaretto biscuits,
  crushed

I love the combination of sweet ripe peaches, raspberries and Amaretto biscuits. This is simple to prepare as you use ready-made pancakes, but good enough to serve at a dinner party.

✳ Preheat the grill.

✳ Lay the pancakes out on a chopping board. Mix the yoghurt, fruit and sugar together in a bowl, spoon the mixture along the middle of each pancake, then roll them up around the fruit. Place the pancakes side by side in a shallow dish, spread the jam over the top and sprinkle them with the crushed Amaretto biscuits.

✳ Place under a hot grill for 4–5 minutes until lightly golden and warm in the middle.

Index

Growing up with Annabel Karmel
Books for every stage of your child's development.

As a parent, giving your child a healthy start in life is a top priority. Annabel offers a cookbook for every stage of your child's development. As the UK's number one bestselling author on cooking for babies and children, Annabel's tried and tested recipes and meal planners have proved invaluable to families for over 20 years.

For more information go to www.annabelkarmel.com

annabel karmel

Acknowledgements

I would like to thank the following for their help and work on this book: Dave King for his beautiful photography; Lucinda McCord for recipe testing; Gwénola Carrère for illustrations; Maud Eden and Lizzie Harris for food styling; Smith & Gilmour for design; Tamsin Weston for props and styling; Liz Thomas for hair and make up; Angus Muir for photography on page 45. Stephen Margolis for eating all the recipes in my book even though his toddler days are a distant memory. My mother Evelyn Etkind for all her support, and for keeping things running smoothly whilst I'm busy creating in the kitchen.

The team at Ebury Press including Fiona MacIntyre, Carey Smith, Sarah Lavelle, Roxanne Mackey, Lucy Harrison, Di Riley and Sarah Bennie. My wonderful models Livi Bayless, Olivia Chambers, Lexie Clarke, Dexter Margolis, Henry McCord and Florence Weston.

Lastly but not least I would like to thank my children Nicholas, Lara and Scarlett for tasting all the recipes.

About the author

Annabel Karmel is the UK's best-selling author on baby and children's food and nutrition. She is the number one parenting author and an expert in creating delicious healthy meals for children without spending hours in the kitchen.

Her previous books have sold more than 4 million copies worldwide and *The Complete Baby and Toddler Meal Planner* regularly features in the top 5 cookery titles.

Annabel was awarded an MBE in June 2006 in the Queen's Birthday Honours for her outstanding work in the field of child nutrition.

Taken from popular recipes from her best-selling books, Annabel's ready-made dishes are taste tested extensively by little ones and created using fresh, natural ingredients, with no added nasties. Perfect for busy mums and dads, the meals are a quick solution to provide your child with nutritious, homemade tasting food. Available in stores nationwide.

Download Annabel Karmel's App
Essential guide to feeding your baby and toddler for lots of recipes, exclusive video content, showing you everything from food preparation to step by step guides and two episodes of Annabel's Kitchen, perfect for keeping little ones entertained!

Available now from the App store & Google Play

www.annabelkarmel.com